TENDER LOVE

GOD'S GIFT OF
SEXUAL INTIMACY

TENDER LOVE

BILL HYBELS

And Rob Wilkins

MOODY PRESS
CHICAGO

ISBN: 0-8024-6349-5

1 3 5 7 9 10 8 6 4 2

Printed in the United States of America

To George and Marianne Lindholm
who have loved us tenderly all these years

CONTENTS

INTRODUCTION

I learned about the mysteries of human sexuality in all the wrong ways. Magazines, the media, and macho friends filled my mind with distorted values and images that took years to erase. This book is an attempt to spare others a similar fate.

For eighteen years I have counseled and wept with people in our church over the tragic consequences of sexual sin. I have done so with a sober awareness that most of us—pastors included—live with an eerie sense that our own sexuality is more complex, powerful, and volatile than we would dare admit. For far too long the subject of human sexuality has been curiously missing from the church's agenda, except for occasional threats and warnings related to its misuse. I wish I could look back on my early years of church attendance and recall stirring sermons on "God's Gift of Sexual Intimacy," or "The Wonder of Human Sexuality." I can't. Hopefully, this book will serve those whose yearning for instruction in this area has never been adequately met.

A clarification may be in order. You will not find, on the pages that follow, a "how to" manual nor a systematic theology of sexuality, though both may indeed have their place. This book explores the *power* of sexuality—the power to unite and the power to divide, the power to enrich the experience of married partners and the power to destroy it.

Once again I have chosen to team up with my friend and fellow-traveler, Rob Wilkins. True to form, Rob couldn't imagine doing a book on the power of human sexuality without incorporating the stories of real people whose sexual journeys mirror the struggles of so many of the rest of us. I owe a deep debt of gratitude to Rob and to those who took the risk of opening up their lives.

As always, my wife, Lynne, provided valuable organizational and editorial coaching for Rob and me. She is gifted far beyond what she is willing to admit.

Working with Greg Thornton and the staff of Moody Press has redefined the concept of enthusiastic teamwork, for which I am most grateful.

And finally, what can I say about the leaders, staff, and congregation of Willow Creek Community Church? For almost two decades they have committed themselves to authentic spiritual development and passionate concern for lost people. Over the years they have been responsible to God's Word and relentless in their desire to apply it to every area of their lives. What a privilege it has been to serve the members of the Willow Creek family and to realize that in spite of all my foul-ups and failures they have continued to move toward me with tender love.

PART ONE

UNDERSTANDING THE CONTEXT

CHAPTER 1

SEX AND GOD

S ex and God.

Just three short words. But juxtaposed they are the source of an enormous sense of tension for many people. Some would say it is even blasphemous to place God and sex so close together. What does sex have to do with God, they ask, and even if there were some kind of loose connection, why would anyone want to cross that bridge?

God is God and sex is . . . well . . . sex. One is holy; the other carnal. One is spirit; the other, loin. The chasm between the two is so great, we believe, it is hard to see them joined by mere conjunction.

GOD AND SEX IN THE CHURCH

Even the church, which should know better, has struggled through the centuries with the connection between God and sex. The world knows this. *U.S. News & World Report*, in an article on sex and Christianity, began: "The history of western religion is a dramatic chronicle of conflict between the sexual and spiritual sides of human nature."[1] Indeed, the church through history has grappled with the role of sexuality. Augustine of Hippo, an early church theologian, believed that sex was the vehicle for transmitting original sin, and therefore corrupt. Pope Gregory I believed that "sexual pleasure can never be without sin." Sex to him was for procreation only. It was best to think of sex as a needful chore, something akin to scaling fish.

Pleasure was out of the question. Between the third and the tenth centuries, the church forbade sex on Saturdays, Wednesdays, and Fridays, as well as during the forty-day fast periods before Easter, Christmas, and Whitsuntide—all for religious reasons. When you add feast days and days of female impurity, one historian estimates that only forty-four days a year were left for marital sex.[2]

Sex for pleasure and emotional well-being is a relatively new idea in Christian history. Thomas Aquinas, the thirteenth-century theologian, as well as the Protestant Reformers John Calvin and Martin Luther, all agreed that sex had purposes beyond mere procreation. But they also viewed sex as somewhat "disorderly." In recent decades, the church has primarily reserved its words about sex to "don't" and "no" and "you better not." In between the negatives, there has been mostly silence. Writes author Tim Stafford:

> In the churches I know, a kid is lucky to get four sessions on sexuality during junior-high or high school youth group. The first three weeks are on dating and how to pick your marriage partner, and the last week there is a little talk about what is really going on— one session, maybe two, to counteract a lifetime of NBC.[3]

GOD AND SEX IN THE BIBLE

The duality of sexuality and spirituality is theologically incorrect. In Greek and Gnostic thought body and soul were separated on the grounds that the physical couldn't be spiritual and the spiritual couldn't be physical. But the Bible does not

14

teach this. It insists that spirituality involves all of what it means to be human—even sex, that seemingly most carnal of acts. There are no apologies or blushes about the issue.

Some of the Bible's strongest illustrations, in both testaments, are sexual in nature. In the Old Testament, a recurring metaphor for Israel was that of a prostitute. "Indeed, on every high hill and under every spreading tree you lay down as a prostitute" (Jeremiah 2:20).

In the New Testament, the church is called the "bride of Christ." The apostle Paul writes: "I promised you to one husband, to Christ, so that I might present you as a pure virgin to him" (2 Corinthians 11:2). The imagery is not accidental. The sexual bond that occurs between a man and a woman in the covenant of marriage—what the Bible refers to as "oneness"—is very much like the intimacy God desires between Himself and His people. In God's design sexuality can never be separated from spirituality, but is meant to be a powerful expression of it.

THE SPIRITUAL ELEMENT OF SEXUALITY

Unbelievers, even those who desperately want to keep God out of their sex lives, can often recognize the spiritual element of sexuality. In a life of time clocks and deadlines, stripped of transcendence, sex has the ring of the divine. Philip Yancey writes: "Probably the closest thing to a supernatural experience my male neighbors have is when they watch actress Michelle Pfeiffer in a clingy red dress atop a piano, or when they pore over each microdot of the annual *Sports Illustrated* swimsuit issue."[4]

God and sex are connected. God *created* sex. For a man and woman in the bond of marriage, sex is designed as a good and powerful gift. It allows them to share with each other the essence of who they are—physically, emotionally *and* spiritually. In an environment of love and commitment, there can be no more powerful expression of exclusive intimacy than sex.

This is true even when a husband and wife are no longer newlyweds. I know of a couple, well into their sixties, who have a dynamic sex life, still feel the fireworks, and literally light up at the idea of giving each other pleasure and intimacy.

15

Don't tell them that sex after sixty is dead because, in many ways, they are only now learning what good sex really involves. They would tell you they are just getting started. They revel in the idea that God has given them such a powerful way to demonstrate self-giving and commitment.

A SEX-SATURATED CULTURE

The world is content with much less.

FBI agent David Ross slips on his trousers in the bedroom of Sally Crane. "I've got to go," he says. "David, don't go," she purrs, "take me around again." She then drops her powder blue dressing gown from her supple body, revealing scanty lingerie. Reclining seductively on the bed, she says, "David, tie me up this time." He hesitates. "Come on, David," she pleads, putting her hand over her head near the bedpost, "tie me up." He gets the picture. And the straps.

Multiple choice question: This scene comes from?

A. An R-rated movie
B. A steamy romance novel
C. Late-night pay television
D. NBC prime time

The correct answer is NBC prime time; the scene was from a mini-series titled "Favorite Son." Times have changed. During the sixties, a couple on television could not be in bed together unless both were fully clothed and one foot of at least one partner was touching the floor. Now, arms and feet are not on the floor but tied to the bedposts.

Television, that nearly omnipresent idol of the electronic age, is increasingly focused on sex. According to one study, a typical network prime-time hour contains an average of 1.6 references to intercourse, 1.2 references to prostitution and rape, 4.7 sexual innuendoes, 1.8 kisses, and 1.0 suggestive gestures. On average, the study says, TV characters today talk about sex or display sexual behavior 15 times an hour—or once every four minutes.[5]

Nearly 90 percent of all those prime-time references to sexual intercourse are referred to outside the context of marriage. And on the September 30, 1992, episode of ABC's "Civil Wars," one of the final barriers was broken: actress Mariel Hemingway bared all for the camera (with her arms draped in strategic positions).

Thinking it would lead us to sexual freedom, our culture has reduced sex to little more than a physical act.

This is the sad state of affairs. Television, which both reflects and creates the moral climate of the country, is clearly displaying an anything-goes attitude when it comes to sex. What is perhaps even more disturbing is that few people seem to be offended. In fact, just the opposite is true. According to another study, 56 percent of adults would find partial nudity acceptable on prime-time TV. Almost 60 percent said that showing a couple under the sheets making love is "OK." More than a third said that full-frontal nudity would not be found offensive to them.[6]

Ours is a world in which Magic Johnson, who has slept with dozens of women, has only one regret: that he had not worn a condom. Even more admired today than when he was a basketball star, he has been elevated by our culture to hero status. Thinking it would lead us to sexual freedom, our culture has reduced sex to little more than a physical act. Despite epidemics of sexually transmitted diseases, the majority of people continue to view sex apart from God's design. Consider the following statistics:

- Nearly 90 percent of college women are sexually active.
- More than 50 percent of all married men and women— some surveys give figures as high as 66 percent—have had

an affair. (The rates for men and women are now virtually identical.)

- The average American has seven sex partners in the span of his adult life.
- Four different nationwide support programs, patterned after Alcoholics Anonymous, have been established for "sex addicts" and boast a membership of more than 20,000.
- There are more hard-core pornographic stores in this country than there are McDonald's outlets.

MADONNA

Sex sells. Ask Madonna. Her book *Sex* sold more than a half million copies in one week. A combination of pornography, sexual fantasy, and sadomasochism, the book featured the blonde superstar exposing herself in front of a window, pulling a man's nipple with her teeth, and hitchhiking naked on a busy Miami street. To say nothing about the naughty stuff.

"The [book] project," wrote *Entertainment Weekly* magazine, "was designed as almost-anything goes, although Madonna and Warner drew the line at pedophilia, violence, and sex with religious objects."[7] In praise of her "restraint," the magazine quoted her stylist as saying, "Madonna is a very moral person."[8]

PORNOGRAPHY

Pornography, much of which makes Madonna look like a virgin, has become a $6 to $8 billion a year industry, most of it controlled by the Mafia and tax free. This is not the kind of air-brushed, seek-and-find pornography most of us grew up with. It is more like raw sewage. Standard fare includes pictures of women being bound and gagged, raped, whipped, and abused. Multiple partners are typical, with homosexual and lesbian layouts a staple item. The underlying theme is usually domination or violence.

And that is some of the tamer stuff available. Other magazines and videos feature every perversion one can imagine (and others that are simply unimaginable): pedophilia; incest; mutilation; gang rape; sex with animals, aliens, and almost any object smaller than a bread box.

PHONE SEX

Pornography has also gone high tech. Phone sex, where a caller pays for the privilege of engaging in a sexually explicit conversation, is a multimillion dollar industry. Again, name your perversion and you will find someone waiting to talk about it: bondage, homosexuality, sadomasochism, whatever. All available through advertisements in most mainstream adult publications. Many of these phone numbers have fallen into the hands of our children, and parents everywhere are finding strange charges on their MasterCards.

COMPUTER SEX

Computer sex is the latest craze. Electronic versions of pornographic magazines, sex clubs, and escort services are available through computer networks at the cost of a few megabytes. Some of the pornographic services are "interactive." The computer user can tell on-screen characters what lewd act to commit. The choices leave little to the imagination.

Software has also gone hard-core. *Time* magazine wrote of the new breed of electronic games:

> Welcome to the world of high-tech titillation, where characters perform feats of on screen electronic eroticism that leave little—or nothing—to the imagination. At the raunchy end of the spectrum are programs like Sexxcapades, which is a sort of kinky Monopoly, and MacPlaymate, in which the player requests a model to remove her clothing and perform graphic acts, complete with audible gasps, grunts and groans.[9]

One such video game (now a series) features a character known as Leisure Suit Larry, who bounces from one sexual escapade to another (fortunately censored on the screen) with well-endowed females bearing names such as Tawni, Bambi, and Passionate Patti. The series did more than $20 million in retail sales in 1991.[10]

Many people predict that computers will eventually do away with sex, or at least provide a highly stimulating alternative. Virtual Reality, a multisensual computer technology, may make it possible for adults to have "sex" over the phone or allow pornography to become extremely user-friendly. A body suit and goggles allow users to enter into a make-believe world (or with a partner linked by another computer) and "make love." Or, better said, "make virtual love." Reports *Time:*

> The way it would work . . . is that you slip into a virtual-reality body suit that fits with the 'intimate snugness of a condom.' When your partner (lying somewhere in cyberspace) [connected through another computer] fondles your computer-generated image, you actually feel it on your skin, and vice versa.[11]

CONDOM OLYMPICS

Condom mania has descended upon us. Everyone knows by now that many schools distribute condoms free to students. Television advertisements show an actor putting a sock on his foot to demonstrate how easy it is to use a condom. One condom company has developed a cartoon character known as "Trojan Man." A company spokesman described the character this way: "He's a larger than life superhero-type person who comes into a variety of different situations and imparts his message in a humorous but very thorough and understanding manner."[12]

In a rather odd twist, many college campuses have recently held "condom olympics," reportedly to lend condoms a "steely image."[13] In Chicago, a store called "Condomplation" recently opened.[14] Guess what it exclusively sells? (If you guessed "philosophical books," you are not only wrong but also a poor speller.)

SEX AS A SALESMAN

Everything in our culture, it seems, has something to do with sex, whether it's our choice in coffee or cars or a cruise line. Sex can still sell about anything. "Jeans," Calvin Klein was quoted as saying, "are all about sssexx." Apparently. In Klein's mind "jeans" must have little to do with jeans. In a recent 116-page ad supplement to *Vanity Fair*, there was lots of sexy stuff, but not much actual denim. *Time* magazine described the supplement this way:

> The thick, glossy portfolio . . . is a jumbled pastiche of naked bodies, black leather jackets, Harleys and tattoos, with cameo roles by

a crying baby and a urinal. Biker chicks straddle their "hogs" and rough up their men. Rippling hunks wield electric guitars like chain saws, grab one another, sometimes themselves. Oh, yes, there are even a few incidental photographs of jeans, most of which are being wrestled off taut bodies or used as wet loin-cloths."[15]

Not all of the advertising industry has been that raunchy. For some, it is equally important that sex be politically correct. Increasingly women are now being pictured as sexual aggressors, rather than available sex objects. The copy line runs something like this: "I just saw what I want for Christmas. And I bet he drinks Johnnie Walker. " Or, in an ad for men's slacks, a winsome model with a coy smile at the corner of her mouth says: "I always lower my eyes when a man passes. To see if he's worth following."

One of the stars of *Basic Instinct*, Sharon Stone, was asked about the graphic violence in the movie, especially the ice-pick murder. She responded: "The murder is a sex act. It's not a violence act."

SEX IN FILMS

Hollywood is still a trailblazer for the distorted and the out-rageous. Although sex continues to flourish in Hollywood, it has, for the most part, endured a bizarre twist, even by Hollywood standards. A whole new genre of films has emerged, called "adult thrillers," which "tap a popular fascination with sexual menace and brutal violence."[16]

Representative of this genre is Tri-Star's $50 million pro-duction *Basic Instinct*. The opening scene of the movie shows a man and woman naked and having passionate sex. Suddenly the woman, on top, ties the man's wrists to the head of the bed, and they continue to make love. As the man reaches orgasm, the woman grabs an ice pick and plunges it time and again into his chest. The camera shows blood splatter across her body.

This is not some back-alley, stiff-lined, cheesy, X-rated movie. It is a major release from a mainstream studio. Increasingly, it is the direction that Hollywood is headed. One of the stars of *Basic Instinct*, Sharon Stone, was asked about the graphic violence in the movie, especially the ice-pick murder. She responded: "The murder is a sex act. It's not a violence act."[17]

SEX AND DEATH

She may be closer to the truth than we might first suspect. In our society, sex is increasingly becoming an act of destruction. And it is not just the AIDS virus that makes it so deadly. Our culture's perversion of God's design for sex—an exclusive and intimate expression of love within marriage—has resulted in predictable consequences. People get hurt and hurt each other. That's what sin does.

As our culture continues to distance sex from our values and our souls, there is an inevitable and terrifying reduction in what it means to be humans made in the image of God. Sex becomes merely a physical act or a wandering thought. Longing attaches itself to pleasure and is unable to handle the load. Addictions set in. Obsessions run wild. The elements God meant for sex to express—commitment, love, spirituality, and oneness—are the very things we destroy by making sex into a one-night stand or a blip on the computer screen. Sex is much like the atom: reduce it and you've got a problem the size of Hiroshima. You end up with lots of destruction and fallout, but no joy.

Sex has become the nineties version of Russian roulette, for individuals and for society. *The Christian Century* perceptively wrote: "Like it or not, many of our most critical problems—divorce, teen pregnancy, abortion, venereal disease, rape, child abuse, fatherless children, abandonment of spouses—are connected to sexual profligacy."[18] What was once called "free

love" has suddenly become considerably more costly, sometimes deadly.

One thing is certain: AIDS has changed the sexual climate.
Once known as "casual," promiscuous sex is surrounded with
fear and danger. More than 120,000 have already died from
complications of the AIDS virus. Experts predict that in the
next two years, more people will die of AIDS than have died of
that disease in the previous ten years.[19]

More than 12 million people contract a sexually transmitted
disease (STD) each year. Our young people, engulfed in a world
snake-charmed by sex, are increasingly at risk. More than 3
million teenagers contract an STD each year, while another 1
million teenage girls become pregnant.[20]

> The church has been lulled to
> sleep. For generations,
> Christian sexual ethics were
> part of the dominant Western
> culture. . . . But times have
> changed. Christians now find
> themselves holding a minority
> position."

The massive push by "safe sex" advocates for the use of condoms is not a genuine solution to the problem. There are at
least two reasons for this. Very few people use condoms. And
the people who do aren't safe. In one study conducted at a California college, it was reported that "less than 20 percent of the
currently sexually active women and men reported using condoms 75 percent of the time or more."[21] Condoms are much
less effective in preventing disease than is usually thought.
Their ineffectiveness in preventing conception is also significant. The failure rate to prevent pregnancy has been reported
somewhere between 15 to 26 percent. To make matters worse

for AIDS prevention, the HIV virus is 450 times smaller than sperm, making it easy for the virus to pass through even the smallest of openings.[22] The Trojan Man, humorous and understanding as he may be, appears to be doomed to failure.

RADICAL SOLUTIONS ARE NEEDED AND WILL CHALLENGE THE CHURCH

Our society's sexual decay will not be reversed without radical change. And this will be difficult. It will be like trying to stop a bowling ball hurtling down an incline: gravity already has the edge. Education won't stop the decline, nor will protest marches slow the downward momentum. New laws won't protect or heal us. Change will only come through a return to truth. A writer for *The Christian Century* states, "[The] real message should be that monogamy, promise-keeping, fidelity and family responsibility are the radical and necessary values of our time."[23]

That brings us back to God. He calls us to be salt and light in the world, preservers and illuminators of the truth. We are not only to speak the truth in love but are to form a pure community—the church—that offers a viable alternative to the culture around us.

WE ARE IN THE MINORITY

But things are not going so well for Christians when it comes to dealing with sexual issues, and speaking truth and providing alternatives are not as easy as they used to be. Stafford writes:

The church has been lulled to sleep. For generations, Christian sexual ethics were part of the dominant Western culture. Not everybody lived by those ethics, certainly, but people generally agreed about what was right and wrong. If a husband cheated on his wife, he didn't say it was the most moral thing he had ever done because for the first time in his life he had been true to himself. He said temptation got the better of him, and everybody agreed it was a shame. That was a comfortable situation for Christians. It is nice to have your views supported by the culture you live in. But times have changed. Christians now find themselves holding a minority position.[24]

The change is not a small one. The tendency is for minorities to become defensive. We often view our differentness as a heavy burden we must grudgingly carry. Staking out a moral position and then defending it is not popular today. We hate to be classed with intolerant bigots; and so, with our backs protected, we often crawl into a corner or a church and hope that no one notices or asks about our standards.

WE HATE TO BE DIFFERENT

I'll never forget a story I read about a woman who attended a meeting where the speaker asked for a raise of hands of those who had committed adultery. As the hands went up all around her, she raised hers also. Why? Not because she had been unfaithful but because she didn't want to be viewed as different. That is an extreme example, but it graphically illustrates the pressure the culture is placing on the Christian community.

The pressure to compromise often feels like a vise grip. For Christians, it is becoming increasingly difficult to take a stand on the issue of sex. Even though many churches now talk openly of sex, even give messages about its being a gift of God, few Christians seem to be willing to live up to God's standards for sex, let alone challenge our culture's values. Perhaps it is a hangover from our heritage, when sex was considered problematic, almost downright embarrassing. Perhaps it is our unwillingness to claim God as the God of sex.

God never intended for Christians to be defensive. He wants us to see our differentness—our uncompromising commitment to truth—as an opportunity for blessing and change. Not to do so will lead to even greater tragedy. When a society is saturated with sexual promptings, addictions, and obsessions and the prevailing philosophy is "If it feels good, do it," disaster is knocking at the door. The family is weakened, the character of our young people is shattered, and lonely, broken people are scattered everywhere like shrapnel. When the church is silent, when no one talks about the enormous consequences of sexual sin, there remains no hope.

We must actively proclaim within our own ranks and especially to our young people that sex was designed to be good and pleasurable, an expression of the highest order, in the bond of marriage. Otherwise we will lose the battle because, in our silence, the decibels of our culture will simply overwhelm us.

WE HAVE OUR OWN SEXUAL HANG-UPS TO OVERCOME

And, of course, we must not become part of the problem. The power of the culture around us must never be underestimated. The often subtle movement in worldviews calls for Christians to be discerning as never before. One of my favorite verses is Jesus' admonition that believers be "as wise as serpents, gentle as doves." When it comes to issues of sexuality, I think that is especially true.

But believers have not always adhered to this standard. In fact, many Christians who have been trapped by the worldly mind-set are now struggling to break free of deep-rooted sexual problems. In studies that differentiate between Christians and unbelievers, sexual behavior has been virtually indistinguishable. According to a *Time* survey of frequent church attenders, only 39 percent of those polled, for example, thought it was wrong for an unmarried adult to have sex.

The Minirth-Meier counseling center in Chicago reports that sexual addiction is the number one reason Christians seek counseling at their clinic; in the last two years, the numbers have exploded.

The problem—the gap between doctrine and behavior—is so severe that several major Christian denominations have considered editing the Bible on the subject of sex. In 1991, the Presbyterians considered abandoning biblical teaching on sex because of a "significant gap between official church teachings and the sexual practices of many people, including many church members."[25] Although the idea was overwhelmingly rejected, it vividly points out a simple fact: it is hard to conduct a revolution when many of your fellow believers are wearing the enemy's uniform or, in this case, no uniform at all.

The world takes notice. Because so many Christian leaders are committing sexual sin these days, one comedian joked that television evangelists should just endorse motel chains instead of freewill offerings.

It's not funny. Increasingly, our churches are being burned by the acid of sexual sin. The church that I pastor is also experiencing the fallout: an alarmingly high percentage of the discipline cases our elders deal with involve some form of sexual misconduct. Sexual ethics, in the place where they are supposed to be the strongest, have clearly been eroded by the culture we are supposed to be changing.

STAYING IN THE BATTLE

There is much at stake in the spiritual battle required today of Christians. Sex has great power. God designed it that way, for our enjoyment. But when it is abused, there are enormous and deadly consequences to pay, as we have already seen. Sex, like few things in life, is intricately and delicately tied to our emotions, our souls, and to who we are. No matter how "casual" sex is, it is always a binding of two into one. When you divide the two back into ones, the process is never accomplished without pain. As one secular psychologist wrote, "Infidelity is for many people the most significant violation of an agreement of trust that can ever affect them."[26]

Where there is deception and despair, the church is mandated to offer truth and hope. Nowhere is this mandate more clearly needed than in the area of human sexuality. But if we hope to lead a revolution, we must have a strategy. We must clearly understand God's design for sex, must be specifically aware of how that plan is under attack, must speak the truth with integrity and compassion, and, most important, must live lives consistent with God's truth. It is only then that we can begin to make a difference in the world around us.

We must not give up. One church leader, urging fellow believers to not yield to the world's values, wrote:

One of the most attractive features of the early Christian communities was their radical sexual ethic and their deep commitment to family values. These things . . . drew many people to them who were disillusioned by the promiscuous excesses of what proved to

27

be a declining culture. Wouldn't it be wonderful for our Church to find such countercultural courage today?[27]

To do so, we must cross that dangerous-looking bridge in our minds. God and sex must go together. For when they are separated, chaos reigns, hearts and lives are smashed, and sex, that most intimate of gifts, becomes cold, wild, and menacing.

NOTES

1. "The Gospel on Sex," *U.S. News & World Report,* 10 June 1991, 59.

2. Philip Yancey, "Not Naked Enough," *Christianity Today,* 19 February 1990, 48.

3. Tim Stafford, "The Next Sexual Revolution," *Christianity Today,* 9 March 1992, 28.

4. Yancey, "Not Naked Enough," 48.

5. Benjamin Svetkey, "Was It Good for You?" *Entertainment Weekly,* 11 January 1993, 20.

6. Ibid., 23.

7. Giselle Benatar, "Sex & Money," *Entertainment Weekly,* 6 November 1992, 20.

8. Ibid., 23.

9. Michael D. Lemonick, "Erotic Electronic Adventures," *Time,* 23 September 1991, 87.

10. Ibid., 87.

11. Philip Elmer-Desitt, "Cyberpunk," *Time,* 8 February 1993, 59.

12. "'Safe Sex' Hurts Kids' Health," *Focus on the Family Citizen,* 20 May 1991, 10.

13. Ibid., 10.

14. "Safer Sex," *Newsweek,* 9 December 1991, 52.

15. Alex Prud'homme, "What's It All About, Calvin?" *Time,* 23 September 1991, 44.

16. "Killer Movies," *MacLean's,* 30 March 1992, 48.

17. Ibid., 51.

18. Walter Benjamin, "Magic and Morality," *The Christian Century,* 4 December 1991, 1127.

19. "Safer Sex," 52.

20. Ibid., 54.

21. Ibid.

22. "Condom Roulette," *In Focus*, 1.

23. "Magic and Morality," 1127.

24. Tim Stafford, "The Next Sexual Revolution," *Christianity Today*, 9 March 1992, 28.

25. "The Gospel on Sex," 63.

26. Beverly Flanigan, "Crimes of the Heart," *Psychology Today*, September-October 1992, 78.

27. "What Does God Really Think About Sex?" *Newsweek*, 24 June 1991, 50.

CHAPTER 2

THE TWO DESIGNS

I would love to be able to run to the corner video store and rent a documentary on the creation of the world. I would fast-forward to the sixth day of creation and watch as God fashioned Adam out of the dust of the earth. Then I would fast-forward to the point where God announced that it was not good for Adam to be alone. I would watch while God put Adam into a deep sleep and created from him the woman named Eve. I would zoom in on the expression on Adam's face when his eyes first saw this new specimen called *woman.*

Obviously, I can't rent that video. Maybe Oliver Stone will make it his next movie project. Until then, I'll just have to use my imagination. I do know that, in a very short time, Adam began to feel something he had never felt before. The first sexual awakening.

What did Adam feel like? Did he sport a sly smile? Did he compliment God on His new creation, something along the lines of "You outdid Yourself this time, God"? One thing was certain: there was a resonance between Adam and Eve that Adam didn't quite know how to handle. With just a little bit of experimentation, however, he soon found out.

The intimacy Adam and Eve shared before the Fall must have been wonderful, more wonderful than intimacy has been ever since, unhindered as it was by the self-serving nature of sin. But we must make love in a fallen world. As sinners we can never fully enjoy the gift but are always destined to distort it, deflecting some of its power into dangerous and destructive paths.

Left to our own devices, in our sexual lives we are like children playing at the controls of a nuclear reactor. We need the vital guidance of the instructions manual: the Bible. In its pages of absolute truth are simple, clear-cut directions on sex. Follow them, and they will lead us to intimacy and sexual joy of incredible power. Ignore them, or create a *Reader's Digest* version—with, say, all the "don'ts" edited out—and we're looking at a meltdown at the core of our souls. It's our choice.

We live in a culture obsessed with and shattered by sex. But that is only the surface problem. The sexual sins of our society are symptomatic of a far deeper trouble: the moral illiteracy of our culture. When it comes to right and wrong, no one cares much for, or is even capable of, reading anything. Not even the writing on the wall. Operating on the premises of an amoral worldview, our culture has adopted a new vocabulary, one that does not include such troubling words as *sin, responsibility, commitment*, and *discipline*.

In a culture obsessed with sex, where virginity and fidelity supposedly belong only to the lonely and to losers, what hope is there for sexual purity? What can Christians do to change the destructive results that always follow promiscuity? Or achieve an even less ambitious goal: keeping themselves from being sexually corrupted by a culture where all is permissible?

My short answer is this: No one promised us a rose garden. The way of Jesus Christ is, at its core, countercultural. Its basic goal—to serve others and to serve God—runs against the grain of the world's purpose statement: *What's in it for me?* Imagine racing the Indianapolis 500 moving in the opposite direction, and you have a vague idea of what the Christian is up against.

In almost every imaginable way, the movement of the world is violently opposed to the surge of biblical truth.

A BATTLE OF WORLDVIEWS

My long answer has to do with strategy, and requires a little background. Jesus said we are in a war, a spiritual battle of monumental proportions. But it is a war unlike most. Although the church has suffered the loss of many martyrs, theirs was a physical death. Now, there is death at another level, on a battleground where the ammunition is ideas and the wounded always die slowly. It is the battle for the mind.

In this clash of perspectives what is at stake has nothing less than eternal consequences. Charles Colson defines the great battle as one between differing worldviews. "This clash of worldviews," he writes, "is at the heart of the great cosmic struggle that rages for the hearts and minds and souls of men and women."[1]

Simply defined, a worldview involves how one perceives the world. The Christian's perspective, based on the unchanging truth of God, is much at odds with the world's perspective, which is constantly in flux. Colson lists several areas of fundamental disagreement:

- The world's view is shaped by the idea that there is no absolute truth (relativism); the Christian's is based on the objective, revealed truth of the Bible.
- The world's view is temporal; the Christian's is eternal.
- The world's view is naturalistic; the Christian's is *super*natural.
- The world's view is pragmatic—do what works; the Christian's is idealistic—do what is right.[2]

It is indeed a peculiar war. The enemies are usually not people, all of whom are offered the grace of God, but ideas. It is all about who gets to define reality. It is about Satan and God. In these terms, sexual behavior is a reflection of a deeper battle over what is right and wrong. If we, as Christians, are to win this war, we must become knowledgeable of those ideas and understand the strategies of the enemy.

Now don't get me wrong. I don't believe that people with overtly evil intentions congregate secretly—say at the United Nations or the Smithville PTA—arguing about the best way to destroy Christianity. I believe Satan is much too clever to be so clumsy and obvious. I am saying that the war over right and wrong in our country is being fought at the level of underlying beliefs that influence behavior. The tools of this warfare are the subtle and interconnected flow of ideas, culminating in value systems. Unless we are aware of the movement of ideas in our culture, and how that movement contrasts with biblical truth, we will be perilously vulnerable to being deceived ourselves. We will fail to win the war because we don't know where to show up for the battles.

SEX, LIES, AND THE TRUTH

But what does all this have to do with sex? Everything. I believe there are very few issues that demonstrate so clear-cut a difference in worldviews. The contrasts are sharp and crisp. The Christian believes in sex in marriage only; the world, for the most part, encourages sexual appetites to be indulged, without boundaries. The Christian views sex on many levels, not the least of which is spiritual; the world often reduces it to a physical act, only sometimes in caring relationships.

The Christian believes that good sex requires a lifelong commitment of love, self-sacrifice, and honesty to one partner; the world believes that sex can be "casual," and places a heavy emphasis on personal gratification and the satiation of appetites. There is at the heart of the difference in worldviews the contrast between self-indulgence and self-giving.

Because the presuppositions of each worldview are so diametrically opposed to one another, it is extremely difficult to cross the yawning chasm with a single verse or thought. People who share no common ground usually end up just screaming at one another. We see it all the time in the debate over today's pressing sexual issues: abortion, homosexuality, condoms and children, and so on.

It's like the man who goes to a foreign country and believes that just by turning up the volume of his voice he will be understood. The problem isn't the number of decibels, it's the vocabulary. Comedian Steve Martin joked about a trip to France, "It's like the French have an entirely different word for *everything*." The vocabulary of Christians often sounds like similar gibberish to those operating under another worldview.

That makes our jobs as witnesses for the good news especially difficult. We must become fluent in the language of both worldviews—the Christian's and the culture's. We must understand the points of connection and difference between the two. And we must be able to translate the truth into changed hearts and minds.

> Although it is impossible to know completely what spiritual intimacy means, I believe that God designed sex as primarily an act of self-giving. This giving of oneself is in some mysterious way irretrievable.

In this chapter, for the sake of clarity we will be describing two worldviews concerning sex. We will examine the consequences of living under "pure" worldviews, which is to say worldviews as they might exist apart from other influences. Of course that's not how reality works; there are many worldviews operating in our culture, each influencing the other. But by examining the Christian's perspective against the dominant worldview, isolated from others, I think we can come to at least an understanding of the *tendency* of thought in our culture.

THE CHRISTIAN'S PERSPECTIVE OF SEX

Even without the video, we know from the story of Adam and Eve that sex was clearly God's design. It did not happen

35

by accident. God made Adam and Eve sexual creatures. He wanted them to revel in sexual pleasure. If He had wanted humans merely to reproduce themselves, He could easily have developed an alternative, more "efficient," system, perhaps some sort of a "baby button" that could be pushed to create a child. Sex was not necessary. In fact, to use the words of an anthropologist, "From an engineer's standpoint, sexual reproduction is insane."[3]

Let's be honest here, what was your first reaction when you found out what sex really involved? Wasn't it something along the line of "You do what?" followed by "You put what where?" followed by "You've got to be kidding. Tell me you are kidding, please, *please!*" Wouldn't you have preferred to do just about anything other than that?

This much is safe to say: if it were left to humans to invent sex, we would probably have come up with a more dignified, prosaic methodology—and missed out on one of life's greatest pleasures. The design of sex reflects creativity beyond human imagination and demonstrates God's character as perhaps none of His other inventions do: playful, given to a little wildness, a lover of passion and energy.

SEX WAS DESIGNED TO EXPRESS INTIMACY OF SOUL

God didn't design sex just to express His love of passion and energy. He designed it so we could experience intimacy. First Corinthians 6:16 states that sexual intercourse unites a man and woman in a "oneness of spirit." In other words, in the arithmetic of sex, $1 + 1 = 1$. The two, in some deep and spiritual way, become one. No other human act or expression has such power or mystery.

This oneness involves more than just the union of bodies. It is designed to be the culmination and consuming expression of a relationship that is growing in love. Only when a man and wife relate to one another at the level of heart and mind, in a trust-filled, open, safe, vulnerable, loving, passionate kind of way, does sexual intercourse represent what it was meant to represent: ultimate unity. Take-your-breath-away intimacy. In that sense what happens between a husband and wife in the kitchen is equally as important as what happens in the bedroom. An environment of trust, love, respect, and security are just as much part of "foreplay" as is a physical caress.

Sex is truly a gift of remarkable depth. It involves intimacy not just on one level, but on almost every human dimension.

SEX WAS DESIGNED FOR PHYSICAL UNION

On the most obvious and superficial level, sex was designed to create a deep level of physical bonding. It is no accident that sexual intercourse actually involves penetration. In a very real sense, one body is joined to another.

SEX WAS DESIGNED FOR RELATIONAL UNION

One of our deepest longings is to be close to someone. Each person wants to connect with another in a tangible way—to enter into that person's experience. Perhaps more than anything else in life sex gives us the opportunity to probe the mystery of who someone else is, while, at the same time, revealing ourselves in the deepest possible way. We become naked before one another, and not just physically. Emotionally, we are also stripped, allowing a level of vulnerability and openness that can in no other way be realized.

SEX WAS DESIGNED TO ALLOW US GREATER SELF-AWARENESS

This concept is vague and somewhat difficult to explain, but there are parallels in other areas of life that help to express it. Just before the Gulf War, I saw young men and women being interviewed about the possibility of facing combat. Most of them said something like this: "I don't know how I'm going to react. But I do know that I'll understand myself better after I've been through combat." When you enter into a sexual relationship within the context of marriage and relational intimacy, your self-awareness increases. Little pieces of your personal puzzle begin to fit into place as you express yourself sexually to another person.

SEX WAS DESIGNED FOR SPIRITUAL UNION

This is the strongest expression of intimacy and the most ignored. Although it is impossible to know completely what spiritual intimacy means, I believe that God designed sex primarily as an act of self-giving. This giving of oneself is in some mysterious way irretrievable. It involves the soul. One man, who was involved in numerous affairs, says later in this book that he "left little bits of myself all over the place." That is the best description I have heard of the spiritual dimension of sexuality.

SEX WAS DESIGNED TO BE RESERVED EXCLUSIVELY FOR MARRIAGE

Sex is a gift from God of incalculable value. The Bible encourages married couples to make liberal use of this gift. First Corinthians 7:4–5 states: "The wife's body does not belong to her alone but also to her husband. In the same way, the husband's body does not belong to him alone but also to his wife. Do not deprive each other except by mutual consent and for a time, so that you may devote yourselves to prayer." In other words, the gift should be enjoyed, each partner giving freely to the other. Christians should see sexuality for what it is: a spiritual and physical celebration between husband and wife, who live together in a partnership designed by God to be a lifelong commitment.

Sex is not to be taken lightly. The Bible is very specific about this. Sex is to be expressed in the context of marriage, in an environment of love, trust, and lifelong commitment. God is serious about this requirement. The author of Hebrews writes: "Marriage should be honored by all, and the marriage bed kept pure, for God will judge the adulterer and all the sexually immoral" (13:4). Ephesians 5:3–5, 1 Thessalonians 4:3–8, and the seventh commandment teach us to avoid all forms of sexual immorality and adultery.

GOD'S RESTRICTIONS LEAD TO FREEDOM AND FULFILLMENT

God demands that sex be limited to marriage for many reasons having to do with His holiness but also because His restrictions in this matter actually lead to our spiritual freedom. God's restrictions call us to a single-minded focus—an exclusivity, if you wish—that may seem oppressive in the short run but leads to greatness in the long run. This general principle, that focus and discipline eventually yield freedom and rewards, is evident in sports. In order to develop the skills, precision, timing, and power necessary to compete at a world-class level, Olympic athletes concentrate on only those activities that contribute to their competitive ability. That almost always involves incredible sacrifice and hard work. It takes nothing less than a lifelong commitment to a single goal. Part of the reason the athletes are so single-minded is their conviction that they have been given a gift of enormous value. It would be irresponsible for them not to develop that gift to its highest potential or to squander it on a series of backyard games.

Sex is like that. For its potential to be fully realized, it must be filtered through a highly focused, disciplined effort. Exclusiveness is required. Intimacy, the highest goal of sexuality, cannot be achieved in ten minutes at a Super 8 Motel. It takes a mutual commitment to a lifelong love; it is only in the security of that unconditional commitment that each partner feels the safety to take the risks of love, self-giving, and vulnerability at the level of the soul. "Will he call me tomorrow?" is not a question that invites the company of intimacy.

Sexual expression in its purest form involves a love that has endured the "dirt" of reality. A couple that has stayed together when circumstances have pushed them beyond the breaking point is a couple that has probed the depths of love. Each spouse understands that love is not a feeling but a commitment to be faithful to one another. It is this discipline of mutual love, pursued in the midst of life's "junk," that affords intimacy its greatest chance to grow. Olympic-standard sex, the very best sex —deeply intimate and focused through years of love—channels its power to make two equal one in a more complete way.

SEX APART FROM GOD'S DESIGN

What happens when you remove the restriction of exclusivity? Disaster. It is like trying to clear out a room full of gas by lighting a match. The whole thing explodes. I can't tell you how often I have witnessed this firsthand in people who have come to me for counseling.

A young woman told me that she and her boyfriend loved each other—*I mean we really, really do*—and that sex for her, even outside the covenant of marriage, was simply a natural expression of their love. A year later, she was calling the suicide hot line, cut to her soul by her boyfriend's betrayal.

A middle-aged man, experiencing a mid-life crisis, justified his one-time fling as "necessary." Something about renewal and self-esteem. He ended up losing his wife, his family, his reputation . . . nearly everything. What remained were guilt and shame.

A teenaged girl, after being told that "everyone does it," decided that she'd better do it. In addition to experiencing a deep sense of disillusionment, she got one of the 4 million annual cases of chlamydia, which, because she was ashamed and afraid to have it treated, led to pelvic inflammatory disease, which rendered her sterile for the rest of her life. And she didn't even really like the guy.

Time and time again, I have seen the physical, emotional, and spiritual damage of sex outside of marriage. Because sex was created by God to be powerful, the consequences of abusing God's design are no less powerful. The wounds that result from sex outside of marriage can leave deep scars. And yet, despite the evidence and just good common sense, people in our society continue to toss out such phrases as "casual sex." Do people really believe that sex can be recreational, no-fault, nonbinding, and uncomplicated? Sex with impunity?

In his book *Why Wait?* Josh McDowell uses a powerful illustration to get at the nature of sexual power—for the good and the bad. A two-year-old boy, cruising through the kitchen of his home, finds a razor-sharp butcher knife on the kitchen table. He picks it up, wrapping his tender fingers around it, and toddles to the family room, where his mom and dad are sitting. The parents are horrified. The father considers leaping off the couch and trying to snatch the knife from his boy's hand. But then he realizes that any sudden movement might make the child grip the knife even more tightly. So he stops and talks very tenderly to the boy, praying that he will understand. Finally, the boy gives his father the knife.

Sexuality, McDowell says, is like that razor-sharp instrument. If used properly, in the context of God's design, it can be a tool for building families and developing long-term intimacy, as well as producing children, who will be raised to be stable and God-fearing, salt and light to the world. If it is abused, it can be a savage weapon cutting deep into heart, mind, and soul. Not to mention the fabric of an entire nation.

The character of the sexual behavior practiced in our culture is clearly damaging—to individuals and to society as a whole. To understand why this damage has occurred, however, requires more than just reciting examples of the aberrant sexual behavior. We must examine the underlying beliefs that permit and encourage that behavior. Until we do so, we will simply be dealing with symptoms, while the disease—a worldview that excludes God—runs rampant.

"IT'S THE CHEMISTRY"

The cover story of the February 15, 1993, issue of *Time* should have come as no surprise. Just in time to make your Valentine's Day, the scientists, anthropologists, and assorted other experts had finally found the secret—make that the formula— of love. With their electron microscopes, statistical findings, and pith helmets, they had finally broken love into its constituent pieces: a combination of genes and chemicals.

Our genes carry the developmental imprint. Over the centuries, love has served the purpose of pulling males and females together into long-term partnerships so that child-rearing was possible. These partnerships were necessary because of the difficulty of caring for an infant at the same time one is gathering food for survival. Explains one anthropologist, "If a woman was carrying the equivalent of a 20-lb. bowling ball [a child] in one arm and a pile of sticks in the other, it was ecologically critical [for her] to pair up with a mate to [help her] rear the young." Point #1: It was necessary for the survival of the species for parents to find a way not to drop the equivalent of a 20-lb. bowling ball.

Chemicals explain the rest of what once was this mysterious thing called love. "Falling in love" is simply the rush of the neural chemicals dopamine, norepinephrine, and especially phenylethylamine (PEA), the scientists tell us. These chemicals are quite similar to amphetamines. Their dominance can last up to two to three years, and then the body begins to build up a resistance.

Further romance, if there is to be any, will have to rely on another set of chemicals. "The continued presence of a partner," the article states, "gradually steps up production in the brain of endorphins." These are natural painkillers, similar to morphine, that "give lovers a sense of security, peace and calm." Proclaims one scientist, "That is one reason why it feels so horrible when we're abandoned or a lover dies. We don't have our daily hit of narcotics."

After the endorphins wear off or fail to kick in, well . . . you're on your own. Unless you can get some help from your oxytocins, that is. Produced by the brain, they sensitize nerves and stimulate muscle contraction. In women, they serve to strengthen uterine contractions during childbirth and also seem to "inspire" mothers to nuzzle their infants. Scientists speculate that oxytocins might also encourage similar cuddling between women and men. They may also enhance orgasms. Point #2: Love is a drug, and you are the drugged.

B ecause we see ourselves as victims, we discard personal guilt for our misdeeds. And that in turn leads to a sense of powerlessness, for when personal responsibility is sacrificed in a society, people give up the ability to exercise free choice in how they respond to life.

And just in case you think you wooed your spouse . . . you guessed it, it was all a setup, a combination of childhood experiences and neural pathways. Each person, we are told, carries in his or her mind a "subliminal guide to the ideal partner," a love map, if you will, which is a record from our childhood of whatever we found enticing, exciting, disturbing, or disgusting.

It could be the way our mothers patted our hair, or the way our fathers swung a bat. A fireman's uniform. A doctor's tongue depressor. Small feet. In-ies or Out-ies. The article states matter-of-factly, "All the information gathered while growing up is imprinted in the brain's circuitry by adolescence. Partners never meet each and every requirement, but a sufficient number of matches can light up wires and signal, 'It's love.'" And here you were thinking that it was your outrageous sense of humor, exquisite physique, and passionate kisses.

So that's it. Love = imprints, chemicals, the ability to carry the equivalent of a 20-lb. bowling ball, and the way your father whistled "Unforgettable." Next mystery, please?

The article in *Time* magazine illustrates in a dramatic way what is wrong with our culture. We have worshiped at the altar of science, and science has told us there is nothing beyond what we can actually see. We can do away with altars, fragrant aromas and hints of spirituality, beauty, love, and transcendence. For whatever cannot be broken down into component parts, seen, felt, analyzed, predicted, and, finally, reduced to a formula is deemed not to exist.

"IT'S JUST PHYSICAL"

In the scientific scheme of things, human beings are nothing but the products of random, and easily disassembled, forces. The mind is only a brain, the body nothing more than a collection of systems, reason simply a million interconnected synapses, and the soul . . . well, it doesn't even stand a chance. For the sake of methodology and ease of study, modern science reduces us in our humanity and makes us less than human.

The act of sex is seen as only physical. Scientists can describe the chemical and neural sequence that produces an orgasm but never even consider the role of spirituality in the sex act. The image of God, a great foggy term for scientific minds, must be removed from sex, for it cannot be "proved."

A LOSS OF VISION

The result is the mess we are in today. Please don't misunderstand: I am not saying that science has been completely devoid of good; it has produced tremendous advancements in medicine; pharmacology; biochemistry; and mechanical, biological, and electronic engineering. There is no question that science has brought about a certain kind of progress; the drop in the mortality rate is proof enough of that. Nor am I questioning the scientific findings reported in the *Time* article cited on previous pages; certainly there are biochemical causes and reactions associated with our attitudes and behaviors. What I am saying is that as beneficial as modern science has been, its achievements have been made possible by the consistent application of aims and techniques that by definition tend to reduce things to the mechanical—and human beings to their biochemical components—and disregard the transcendent.

Science is concerned with observation, not the meaning of what it observed. In itself it cannot provide a worldview. Yet we have looked to science to do so. Manifold consequences have come from this mistake, some of which are listed below.

A Victim Mentality

As science and technology continue to dissect humanity, so-called evidence is put forth to prove that we are not responsible for our own behavior. As we have seen, love is described as nothing more than the predetermined movement of imprints, chemicals, and neurological maps. Fat, according to a recent *Psychology Today*, is mainly a genetic predisposition. Alcoholics are the victims of a bad gene. Homosexuals are wired for same-sex impulses. People who steal do so because they have been robbed of their childhoods. And all of us, to one extent or another, are seen as the victims of our parents, our potty training, too much sugar, or bad television.

Since science does not have to do with the invisible and impenetrable realities of will, conscience, soul, and even reason itself, all of which are counterweights to the determinism just described, science has concluded that we have no responsibility for our lives but are only controlled. We can respond but are not responsible. For to be responsible would require us to have the ability to love and to hate, to distinguish right from wrong, and to understand the difference between wisdom and information—all capacities of individual initiative not accounted for in a mechanistic universe.

To admit that we are responsible would require acknowledging the existence of mystery. And that is something modern man will not do, for mystery, something revealed to man and which he does not fully understand and cannot "enclose" or tame through technology, might lead to the assumption that we are made in the image of God, that great unseen, unaccountable, unbreakable Spirit.

Consequently, we have concluded that we can do no better than to be content—"contentment" being that certain feeling produced by the release of certain chemicals—with being victims. The psychological overspill of such thinking is immense and clearly visible in our culture. Because we see ourselves as victims, we discard personal guilt for our misdeeds. And that in turn leads to a sense of powerlessness, for when personal responsibility is sacrificed in a society, people give up the ability to exercise free choice in how they respond to life. As physician Dean Ornish puts it, "The flip side of [responsibility] is to say that you . . . are just a victim of fate, or bad genes, or bad luck. If you're just a helpless victim, there's not much you can do about your condition."[4]

Helplessness, in turn, leads to seeing the world in terms of personal "rights" to be demanded and not in terms of gifts to be accepted. The thinking goes like this: *Since I am a slave to my genes, neurons, and imprints, I am not responsible for my own welfare; therefore, others must provide my needs for me. These needs—make that rights—include sexual expression. I am owed the satiation of my sexual drives and therefore am justified in taking them as I please.* In this worldview, sex is not a matter of giving but of getting, and sexual responsibility and accountability drown in a sea of personal demands.

The LOSS OF TRUST AND MORAL AUTHORITY

Communication theorist Neil Postman argues brilliantly in his book *Technopoly* that science and technology are destroying our culture.[5] Postman defines "Technopoly" as the value system, founded on scientific thought and technique, that gives technology free reign, even though technology in itself is devoid of guiding principles. He writes, "Abetted by a form of education that in itself has been emptied of any coherent worldview, Technopoly deprives us of the social, political, historical, metaphysical, logical, or spiritual bases for knowing what is beyond belief."[6]

At one time scientists studied nature to understand better how God designed the universe. That kind of scientific study acknowledged the transcendent. But modern science is practiced as an end to itself. By its very nature it cannot tolerate that which is transcendent. This devastates our culture. Postman correctly notes: "No culture can flourish without narratives of transcendent origin and power. The alternative is to live without meaning, the ultimate negation of life itself."[7]

In a culture dominated by scientific reasoning, facts and information replace truth. That is a necessity, for again, within the perspective of modern science, truth is impossible and irrelevant. It is impossible because it contains transcendent elements; it is irrelevant because we are not responsible for or even capable of living by the standards of truth, if indeed such a thing as truth exists.

The scientific worldview, with its emphasis on what can be measured and observed, is at odds with Christianity—not because the science "disproves" Christianity—but because, by definition, faith is "being sure of what we hope for and certain of what we do not see." Faith deals with hope and transcendence: two great antonyms of scientific determinism and the quantifiable. The scientific worldview, in its purest form, cannot address Christianity because, to use Ornish's pithy expression, it assumes that "if we can't measure it, it doesn't exist, and it's not real."[8]

When only the measurable is acknowledged, absolute truth, which encompasses both the measurable and immeasurable, is the first casualty. Relativism then becomes the dominant force in the culture—and that is what has happened in our society. We have dismissed the truth of Christianity and in so doing have lost the source of truth and moral authority. We have cut ourselves off from principle and experience a sense of alienation and weightlessness.

RELIANCE ON THE HERE AND NOW

When truth becomes relative and absolute standards are abandoned, there is no reason for objective interpretation of history, law, or politics. Past events and writings are seen as meaningless. The effect is to cut ourselves from the anchors of history, leaving ourselves to float in the universe. And without the compass of history, it is impossible to predict a future.

What is left is Now, the timeless moment. Our secular (which means "of this present age") society is enamored with such slogans as "Carpe diem" (Latin; "pluck the day"; often given as "seize the day") and the Pepsi commercial's advice to partake in the "Right Now." We are attached to the idea of instant gratification—especially when technology provides us with more and more quick fixes. Aspirin, antacids, and antihistamines are advertised not so much on the basis of long-term effectiveness, but on the basis of how quickly they begin to work.

> The overwhelming consequence of adopting the worldview of science is a loss, collectively and individually, of intimacy. . . . We have disconnected ourselves from responsibility, absolute truth, history, . . . and morals.

We have fast foods, instant banking, rapid tax returns, quick marts. Value is judged by seconds, even less. People will pay top dollar for a computer that can process information a few extra nanoseconds faster.

Yet, in the rush of the instant, deeper problems are often ignored. This is most dramatically seen in the way we pursue good health. Says Ornish, "To get a quick fix, we will try [any medical procedure] and yet . . . avoid looking at our own behaviors and at what underlies [them]. But if we want real healing, we will have to address the deeper issues."[9] Those deeper issues, he believes, are such things as the need for community, intimacy, and belonging—the very things that science cannot fully understand, let alone provide.

In a quick-fix environment, critical values, such as discipline, patience, temperance, and moderation, to name just a few, are easily discarded as irrelevant or incomprehensible. It is not surprising that sex is often viewed as a god of Carpe Diem. Too much stress? Unwind with a little sex. Low self-esteem? Prove yourself attractive in bed. A wife who doesn't understand you? Find a little tenderness wherever you can. On the surface, sex offers quick relief without dealing with more troublesome realities.

THE RULE OF WHAT IS EFFICIENT

Without the anchors of truth and context, ours is a culture that, as Francis Schaeffer put it, "has its feet firmly planted in mid-air." Rarely does someone ask, "What is true?" but, more often, "What will work for me?" In a culture reduced to scientific reasoning, what is efficient replaces what is moral. Postman writes:

> The Technopoly story is without a moral center. It puts in its place efficiency, interest and economic advance. It casts aside all traditional narratives and symbols that suggest stability and orderliness, and tells, instead, of a life of skills, technical expertise, and the ecstasy of consumption.[10]

If something isn't working efficiently, just get rid of it: a garbage disposal, a work ethic, your wife. Pragmatism, with its cold and calculating sense of reason, has become the dictatorial god of our age.

THE LOSS OF INTIMACY AND CONNECTEDNESS

The overwhelming consequence of adopting the worldview of science is a loss, collectively and individually, of intimacy.

We have allowed science, in the name of efficiency and formula, to reduce humanity to a set of neurons, chemicals, and
synapses. We have disconnected ourselves from responsibility,
absolute truth, history (except as it is contained in our evolu-
tionary implants), and morals. We are, as Walker Percy put it,
"lost in the cosmos."

Yes, there still exist, even in our unbelieving world, hints of
truth, whispers from our past, and the light of conscience. But
these are the survivors of the scientific worldview, not its
products. Pure science, usurping past its rightful boundaries,
cannot tolerate those concepts. In such an environment, the
tendency is always toward disintegration and reductionism.
We become disconnected from ourselves and from others.

In the resulting chaos of scientific facts, information, theories, data, news reports—unfiltered through any scheme of values or transcendent ideas or truth—the individual is removed
from belief, a sense of coherency, and, I believe, from others. It
is not so much the stress, but the isolation. Writes Ornish:

> People tend to think about modern culture as somehow more
> stressful because we have fax machines and cellular phones, and
> because modern life is so much more fast-paced. But our ancestors
> had to wonder whether the crops were going to come in, or wheth-
> er their children were going to die of polio before they reached the
> age of thirteen. Clearly, that has to be as stressful as whether the
> fax has come in on time. But something has changed. What is dif-
> ferent now is that cultural isolation is so pervasive in our culture.
> We used to have extended families, and at the church or syna-
> gogue or workplace or in the neighborhood we felt a sense of safety
> and community. We often don't have that now. Two-parent house-
> holds are the exceptions rather than the rule. There aren't many
> places where people can feel safe enough just to be who they are
> without having to create a mask or a facade to experience the inti-
> macy and the community that we are all looking for.[11]

Those places people normally go for a sense of intimacy—
marriage, family, church, and community—are all in the process of deterioration under the scientific worldview. More than
half of all marriages now fall apart, which results in a splinter-

ing of the family. Few people attend church, and most don't even know the name of their next-door neighbor.

Such a break-up of society further reduces the possibility of intimacy. For example, the April 1993 issue of *Atlantic Monthly* stated that "recent research shows that many children from disrupted families have a hard time achieving intimacy in a relationship, forming a stable marriage, or even holding a steady job."

THE RISE OF MYSTICISM AND
A FUTILE SEARCH FOR THE TRANSCENDENT

Science defines the world as cold, calculating, and reducible. It sees humans as products of evolution, mere signs that the species still continues, and beings predisposed to love, that predetermined emotion of fired synapses and released chemicals. I believe that the current fascination with New Age religion and other cults is a direct reaction to fragmentation created by the scientific worldview. In order to recapture what is missing in their world, these religionists are bent on the other extreme: a fascination with mysticism, the emphasis on the nonrational and the touchy-feely-we-are-one-with-the-world mind-set. There is an almost desperate attempt to recapture transcendence and intimacy from the steely, clawlike hand of science.

DEPRECIATION OF OUR SEXUALITY

Despite such New Age attempts, science still defines much of our culture's cold reality. Which brings us to our central question: in such a prevailing worldview, what happens to our sexuality? I'll start by repeating what has already been said in this book: it is next to impossible, outside of faith, to realize God's design for sex—intimacy in the context of an exclusive covenant of marriage. Sex, in the prevailing worldview, is indulgent, instant, physical, and free from moral boundaries. Not surprisingly, it is also usually disconnected from commitment, sacrifice, spirituality, and lifelong love. Intimacy, on a good day, lasts about twenty-five minutes.

But that's an oversimplification. Sex is much too powerful to reduce, even by the best of scientific techniques. Because the force of our sexuality is so strong, it cannot, I believe, be fully disconnected from the truth. By instinct and experience, people know that sex was meant to be something more than a physical act. Information and facts, even from a gynecologist, cannot reduce the mystery of sex. In a world of concrete facts and split atoms, where everything is quantifiable and knowable, such a whisper of transcendence has a powerful voice.

RESORT TO THE EXTREMES OF FEAR AND LUST

In a broken-down world, sex invites two extremes: avoidance or worship. The first has to do with fear; the second, lust. In *The End of Sex*, George Leonard maintains that sexuality, with its powder kegs of guilt and disillusionment, is simply not worth the trouble. Add on top of that the fear of disease, a broken heart, and a failed marriage or two, and sex simply makes people too vulnerable.

The other extreme is excess. The attitude toward sex today is often one of worship. The thirst for intimacy and transcendence, lacking better options, gets routed into the closest thing many can come to a miracle: sex.

When intimacy and community disappear from a culture, sexuality is often pushed past its limits. It is like a starving man who, finding no real food, eats a handful of dirt because, if nothing else, it temporarily fills his stomach. Because such sex is mostly disconnected—from values, partners, and the movement of life—it often leads to promiscuity. It is the act of sex that matters. Promiscuity of this kind is, as Philip Yancey phrases it, "a modern mutation of classical idolatry, a commitment of spirit to something that cannot bear its weight."[12]

Today, we call it addiction. Addiction is rampant in our society—addictions to everything from chocolate to shopping to work to gambling to sex. Thousands of support groups across the country seek to help people break through the prisons of their addictions, which often cost them their health, self-esteem, and bank accounts. The development is not at all surprising. In a world where God is relegated to myth, people are trying to find something, anything, to fill their lives with meaning and unconditional intimacy. The problem is this: God cannot be replaced. Any attempts to do so will lead to devastation.

SEARCHING FOR A HIGHER LOVE

People want—need—a love that transcends the definable. They thirst for intimacy, for a spiritually pure love. Here is a connection point for talk of spiritual matters. It gives us a bridge to go beyond judgment and jargon to an act of restoration.

Jesus was a master at this type of conversation. Chapter 4 of the book of John tells of the meeting between Jesus and a Samaritan, who, in the words of Yancey, was "a California-style woman who had already ditched five husbands and who liked to stay current on the latest religious trends."[13]

When Jesus meets her at a well, He masterfully connects her physical thirst to a thirst for something much deeper. He recognizes her marital meanderings as desperate attempts to fill a void in her life. Instead of looking to God to fill that need, she was attempting to find a human relationship that could never do what she desired. In one penetrating and, at first, confusing statement, Jesus gets at the heart of the matter: "Everyone who drinks this water will be thirsty again, but whoever drinks the water I give him will never thirst."

When it came to reaching people with the good news—that thirst and hunger can be permanently satisfied through him—Jesus sought to be aware of the context of the lives of individuals. That was what the Incarnation was all about. Of course, He had advantages. He knew sinlessly and intuitively about the hearts of men and women. We, being limited by sin and perspective, must work harder. But whatever our limitations, we need to present the gospel in the context of each individual life and the cultural environment in which people make decisions. Without such connections, we risk offering truth in a vacuum.

But redeeming the culture is not the only valid reason for knowing the thoughts of the unsaved and the worldview of our culture. Such knowledge not only helps us to penetrate our world but also gives us some protection against destructive influences. As we move on to Part Two of this book, we will examine our sexual journeys as well as some protective measures we, as Christians, can take to become or remain sexually pure.

As we will see, the church has been deeply penetrated—raped, if you will—by the world's "values" in the area of sexuality.

In many cases we have accommodated the culture because we have remained uninformed about the strategies and thinking of the enemy. If we are specifically unaware of the dangers we are up against, we will be like boxers in a heavy fog with only two equally disastrous choices: flail our punches wildly at whatever may be out there or curl up in a corner and pray for the best. One leads to exhaustion; the other to isolation.

We can afford neither reaction. For if the way we see our sexuality is to impact our own lives and our society and expand the kingdom, we must live the way God wants us to—with sexual purity and sexual joy. We will not be heard, no matter how effective our strategy, until we can be seen living out God's design.

NOTES

1. Charles Colson with Ellen Santilli Vaughn, *The Body* (Dallas: Word, 1992), 184.

2. Ibid., 194.

3. Anthropologist John Tooby of the University of California at Santa Barbara as quoted in "Is Sex Really Necessary?" *Time*, 20 January 1992, 47.

4. Dean Ornish, as quoted in Bill Moyers, *Healing and the Mind* (New York: Doubleday, 1993), 102.

5. Neil Postman, *Technopoly: The Surrender of Culture to Technology* (New York: Alfred A. Knopf, 1992).

6. Ibid., 58.

7. Ibid., 172.

8. Quoted in Moyers, *Healing and the Mind*, 104.

9. Ibid., 113.

10. Postman, *Technopoly*, 179.

11. Quoted in Moyers, *Healing and the Mind*, 106.

12. Philip Yancey, "Not Naked Enough," *Christianity Today*, 19 February 1990, 48.

13. Ibid., 48.

PART TWO

EXPLORING OUR SEXUAL JOURNEYS

CHAPTER 3

DISCOVERY

When I was in high school in the sixties, I was part of a subculture that revolved around cars. The sure ticket to popularity was a high performance machine with a couple hundred horses under the hood. Our lives revolved around those cars: many of us took two or three jobs to be able to cruise in the right one. On weekends, we raced them on the back streets; during the week, we earned money to provide the costly maintenance. We all tried to outdo one another with big engines, loud pipes, and huge tires.

But there was more to it than *what* we drove. There was also *how* we drove. What could we do with our car that would make us stand out from the crowd?

A friend of mine came up with a particularly effective method of drawing attention to himself. He disconnected the brake lines to his rear wheels and put extra-heavy-duty brake pads on his front wheels. Then, at midday, he would wait in the high school parking lot until the lunch hour, when all the students gathered for daily drag races or other meaningful activities.

When the moment was just right, my friend would put his car into first gear, rev up the engine, and push his foot almost to the floor. The machine would scream, making all sorts of noise. Next, he would pop the clutch, jam his left foot on the brake, and push the accelerator to the floor.

This created an amazing phenomenon. The back tires would spin like crazy and smoke would pour out of the rear wheel wells, while the front tires would be locked. He would travel at about five miles per hour around the parking lot with the whole car lurching up and down, screaming and smoking. The front tires would smoke because they were skidding, and the back tires would smoke because they were spinning. He'd vibrate around, and everyone would clap.

One day he started his performance with the usual big crowd gathered around. He revved the engine, popped the clutch, and jammed the brakes. As usual, the car started hopping, vibrating, and smoking. But he had done it one time too many. There was too much stress on the drive train; the drive shaft disintegrated and parts from it began bouncing across the parking lot. Parts flew everywhere like shrapnel, trashing the undercarriage of his car. The power, once a source of wonder and envy, had now become a destructive force.

POWER GONE AWRY

Sexual activity can be like that, particularly when we first begin to discover its power. Is it any wonder that in the teenage years, bolstered by the hormone of Near Omniscience, our sexuality has the potential to cut us deeply, leaving scars that can last a lifetime?

Set against the frequent confusion, alienation, and anonymity of the adolescent era, the deep and powerful sense of intimacy, acceptance, and love that sex promises can become a critical motivator to young people. They can easily see sex as the antidote to relational hunger. In an environment of immaturity and deep need, they are like my friend in his car, trying anything, no matter how costly, crazy, or dangerous, just to be recognized.

It does not take an Einstein to recognize the potential for abuse. There are nearly 1 million teenage pregnancies each year, many of which end in abortion. At the same time, another 3 million teenagers contract a sexually transmitted disease. In fact, by the time the sexually active teenager graduates from high school, he or she has a one in four chance of contracting an STD. That is to say nothing of AIDS, or the emotional and relational catastrophes that all too often follow misused sex.

EDUCATION OUT OF BALANCE

A major contributing factor to this kind of pain, I believe, is flawed sex education: we simply don't tell our children enough. We err in two ways in this, adopting two equally dangerous extremes: embarrassment and arrogance. The first is often practiced by caring families, many of them Christian, who are embarrassed by or confused about sexuality. It is simply too difficult for them to talk about. What often happens, if anything at all, is that the adults will emphasize the negative aspects of sexuality to their children, giving them rules without reasons.

The other extreme, often practiced in seventh-grade health classes (but sometimes even in the home), is arrogance. This attitude grows out of the prevailing belief, generated by the worldview of naturalistic science (see chapter 2), that sex is nothing but a physical act. Too often we stop at body parts, statistics, and warnings. We just don't make the effort to teach the larger context of sex.

Teachers who have this mind-set present detail after detail concerning the physical act, including explicit diagrams and often videotapes, but leave untouched the relational, emotional, and spiritual dynamics of sexuality.

On the one hand, children learn that sex is a collection of rules that, like all rules presented apart from a context, create a sense of mystery and encourage rebellion, curiosity, and experimentation. On the other hand, they learn that sex is something physical and uncomplicated, like doing push-ups. Unaware of the harmful consequences, they adopt a "playful" view of sex that too often leads them to experiment with a destructive game. Both extremes need to be balanced by the Word of God.

Rebecca, a fifth grader, was sitting in the big chair in her family's living room, watching television. She felt a tap on her shoulder. Her mom, looking somewhat tense, had reached around the planter to get Rebecca's attention. She motioned her toward the bedroom door. After the bedroom door was shut and locked, Rebecca's mother pulled a book down from the top shelf of the closet. Together, they lay down on the bed and examined it.

The first twenty pages or so were about having a period. They moved through them fairly quickly and without tension. As they neared the end of their conversation, Rebecca noticed that the pages of the next chapter of the book had been stapled together. She knew, almost instinctively, that those pages were about sex. Her mom just barely mentioned it. Rebecca remembers her words clearly: "Sex is a beautiful thing," she said, "a holy thing." Well, if sex is so holy, Rebecca remembers thinking, why are those pages stapled together?

That was the way it was between Rebecca and her parents: protection was often equated with ignorance. Her parents, she believes, wanted what was best for her, even though that "best" had little or no connection with reality. They were strict, religious people and built their world on rules. Anything that did not fit—either a sassy mouth or a sinful thought—was quickly relegated to nonexistence. There was no room for discussion or questioning. Once a friend told Rebecca that her dad and mom took showers together. When Rebecca told her mom what the little girl said, her mom responded by saying, "No, people don't do that."

Rebecca heard about intercourse for the first time in high school. It is not surprising that she found it unbelievable. It was about the same time that her dad, who never said any-

thing *about sex, looked up over his newspaper in the morning and said to his daughters, "You girls know that French kissing is like oral intercourse and is wrong, don't you?" Then he returned to his newspaper.*

Rebecca's parents tried their best to create a safe environment for their children. But, at the same time, Rebecca remembers a stiff coldness in the family, a relational distance that could not overcome a fear of the unknown or unexpressed. Her father had had a tough childhood; he had quietly grieved over the deaths of loved ones, to whom he was extremely close. "Tenderness," Rebecca says of her father, "seldom surfaced." The rules held back the pain.

Sex became a paradox of sorts for Rebecca. Not dirty, but forbidden. Her parents were afraid of Rebecca. She liked clothes, music, parties, dating. She flirted with the edges of the barriers her parents established, not so much out of rebellion but for the sake of self-expression.

She lived in a state of curiosity combined with fear. Her parents worried about her purity. One time, when she was twenty and still a virgin, she went fishing with a boyfriend. Her father had laid out the fishing rods, but she forgot them. They used her date's poles instead. When she came home, about midnight, the door to the front door flew open. Her father was in a rage. He accused her of not fishing, hurled a flowerpot at her head, and called her a whore. It took him a week to apologize.

Besides the hurt of feeling untrusted, Rebecca began to wonder: What was there about sex that could generate such horror?

George Michael's song "I Want Your Sex," with its repetition of the blunt request stated in the title, went to the top ten on the pop charts. It's a long way from "I Want to Hold Your Hand." It is written, in fact, for a different world. Whereas most of us worried about how to improve our jump shot or make enough money to buy a Stingray bike, our children face an entirely new and often overwhelming definition of fun and games. Role models such as Michael and Madonna send the

61

message, over and over: indulge. If you are physically ready for sex, you are ready.

Many of our children feel pressure to have sex before they are prepared. Recently a network television news show reported that, in one high school, star student athletes had made sexual conquest a game. For each sexual adventure, points were awarded. The students kept track of each other's sexual activity, just as one scores a football game. The competition was intense. Those who scored poorly or chose not to play were scorned.

Billboards, magazines, television, and movies bombard our youth with sexual images, leaving them sexually alert but ignorant of, or desensitized to, the consequences. Sex and violence are the two overriding themes. While standing in a line at a movie theater, I heard a teenaged boy say, "If this flick doesn't have a whole lot of skin and blood in it, I'm not even going."

In the eighties, a whole genre of "slasher" movies—*Friday the 13th* and *Nightmare on Elm Street* being the most popular— offered our children decapitations, dismemberments, and murders with ice picks and chain saws. Today, VanDamme and Schwarzenegger kick, punch, and shoot their way through human bodies like sharks through a school of guppies.

The same kind of violent transformation is happening to sex. Through saturation of images and acts, sex is reduced to the commonplace, stripped of love and consequences, and offered as little more than a naked pursuit of orgasm, the ultimate instantaneous pleasure.

It's gotten to the point that "abstinence" has become synonymous with "impossible." Sexual experts tell us it isn't realistic to expect our children to refrain from sexual intercourse. That's a message today's kids are pleased to hear. Living in a world of increasing isolation and alienation, often coming from broken homes, they are eager to give the Hollywood kind of sex a whirl. Why not, when it seems to offer unbelievable pleasure and no negative consequences? At younger and younger ages, children barely able to recognize their budding sexuality are engaging in sexual intercourse. A survey in one high school system revealed that 55 percent of all junior high students had already had sex.

The pressure begins at an even younger age. My son, Todd, attended a good Christian elementary school. One day in fourth grade he came home upset about a friend who had gotten into trouble for punching a kid. When my wife asked him what caused the fight, Todd said, "For two weeks four boys in my class have been bugging my friend to have sex with a girl in our class." His friend couldn't make them stop, so he slugged one of his tormentors. Those were fourth-graders. In a good Christian school, they were taunting one another to have sex.

Only after it is too late do many children realize the fantasy of such casual and ignorant notions about sex. Their lives are often destroyed through teenage pregnancies, wounded hearts, and shattered hope. Sex becomes a knife that cuts away the things they desire most: self-esteem, respect, and intimacy.

Christian parents often feel they are in a losing battle. We cower under the pressure, confused about what to do and unsure of what to say. The result is that, when it comes to sex, our kids seek advice from others.

In a *Young Miss* survey, 66 percent of 4,000 teenagers surveyed said they avoided discussing sex with their parents. This lack of communication in families is deadly. We as parents must take the responsibility and pour creative energy into opening lines of communication and addressing the critical issues related to our children's sexuality.

JUST SAY IT

We all know that talking about sex is more difficult than it sounds. When my daughter, Shauna, was three years old, she made a curious discovery. I was in the bathroom after taking a shower and the door was not quite shut. Shauna cruised by and did a double-take. She stopped, backed up, and asked, "What's that, Daddy?" Being the mature, well-adjusted, open-minded father that I am, I called out for my wife.

By our actions (or lack of actions) children quickly learn there is a mystique about sex. We need to learn a balance between making sex overly mysterious and loading down our children with unnecessary facts. In our conversations about sex, we should be honest, simple, and direct. We must not avoid questions (as I did in the previous paragraph!). And we should always take advantage of spontaneous opportunities to discuss sexuality with our children, even if the child's expression of sexual interest is awkward or inappropriate.

One of those occasions came up at small, very quiet restaurant where our family had stopped for breakfast. Two businessmen sitting at a table next to us were the only other people in our area of the dining room. The waitress brought our menus and then left. As she was leaving, Todd, three at the time, said without embarrassment, "Gee, dad, she has big boobs."

The two businessmen nearly fell off their chairs laughing. I attempted not to panic. I knew this was an important moment in my son's life, so I took him aside and said to him, "Son, your dad noticed that, too. It's OK to notice that type of thing. But girls get embarrassed if you talk about it, so it's better to talk about that sort of thing when we are alone." I did not want to shame him or deny his natural and God-given sense of curiosity.

AFFIRM SEXUAL DEVELOPMENT

If the process of sexual development is faced alone or in the context of a strict-rules mentality, guilt and fear are often the result. A "wet dream," for example, may be interpreted by a young boy as punishment from God for masturbation. A girl who matures more slowly than her classmates may feel guilty, fearing that her lack of development is punishment for having sexual feelings.

What we say or how we react to our children's sexual development can do tremendous good or nearly irreparable harm. Recently, I read about a man who was receiving counseling because he found it difficult to be sexually intimate with his wife, especially when it came to intercourse. In counseling, he revealed an incident that happened to him when he was twelve.

He was in the bathroom, masturbating. He had just started having erections and was curious about the feelings he was experiencing. While he was experimenting, his father walked in on him. He reacted in shock and anger: "If I ever catch you doing that again," he screamed, "I'll break every bone in your body. You will bring yourself to ruin."

In that boy's mind, the thought took root: *manipulation of my penis will lead to ruin.* Well into his marriage, that fear overwhelmed his sex life.

> S ex education must begin by first demonstrating, then teaching, the power of loving relationships. Through our words and actions, we must familiarize our children with the vocabulary of relationships: love, honesty, intimacy, forgiveness, and grace.

We must take great pains to help our children see their developing sexuality as wonderful and God-given. When our grade school kids develop "crushes" on friends, we should say, "Hey, that's a healthy thing. God built you to feel that way." As our children grow older, we should continue to affirm their increasing fascination with the opposite sex, so they don't grow up suspicious of their sexuality.

One survey revealed that less than 10 percent of boys and girls "have had discussions with their parents or other responsible adults who could help them accept sex as *normal* and *natural.*" As a result, they begin to develop deep feelings of shame and guilt for just experiencing sexual feelings and thoughts. We must teach our children that those feelings and thoughts are not wrong—God designed us to function that way. What is important is what we do with those feelings and thoughts.

CREATE AN ENVIRONMENT OF LOVE

Sex must always be taught and learned in the context of relationship. To be made in the image of God means to be relational, for God is three persons in unity: the Father, the Son, and the Holy Spirit in perfect relationship with one another.

Sex education must begin by first demonstrating, then teaching, the power of loving relationships. Through our words and actions, we must familiarize our children with the vocabulary of relationships: love, honesty, intimacy, forgiveness, and grace. If a child never learns this vocabulary, he or she will not have the tools to understand that sex is meant to be an expression of a loving, intimate relationship.

Another reason for providing an environment of love for our children is that the greater the child is loved, respected, and valued at home, the greater the possibility that he or she will not get involved prematurely in sexual activity. A child who is loved at home has a deep sense of security and acceptance that acts as a sort of protective shield.

In contrast, a child who feels unloved at home is more likely to see sex as the answer to unmet needs for intimacy, self-esteem, and acceptance. He will risk almost all dangers to find what he instinctively knows is missing. This pursuit will inevitably end in devastation and deep wounds.

There are no guarantees, of course. Raging hormones, unsettled emotions, and the awkward, confusing transition from childhood to adulthood sometimes sends children from even the most loving homes off into the wilderness of promiscuity where anything can happen. But, with a sense of love and intimacy at home, that *anything* is far less likely to happen.

COMMUNICATE GOD'S DESIGN FOR SEX

Taking these steps will be helpful. But they will still fall short, for they deal with superficial issues. What is needed if our children are eventually to enjoy sex in the way that God intended is for them to know God's design for sex. Some aspects of that design have been given earlier in this book:

- Sex was designed to express intimacy of soul
- Sex was designed for physical union
- Sex was designed for relational union
- Sex was designed to allow us greater self-awareness

- Sex was designed for spiritual union
- Sex was designed to be reserved exclusively for marriage
- God's restrictions lead to freedom and fulfillment

Brad's story illustrates how difficult it is for parents to teach their children about God's design for sex, and it brings up other elements in God's design for sex.

In his childhood world, Brad had it all: five acres of land, some of it wooded, a dog named Trots, a sandbox for creating other planets, two brothers, and all the love that his dad and mom could give him, which was significant. He wouldn't have used the word back then, but what he felt was safe. He can still remember the way his father's voice sounded on an October evening, calling him in for supper. Brad's world was full of excitement—monsters in the weeds, aliens in the Lego village, and Johnny Bench in the backstop—yet he felt secure. He was free to pursue childhood with all of his childlikeness.

In many ways, his family was typical of the homes of the sixties: Dad—strong, decision maker and breadwinner; Mom—funny, submissive, and bread maker. Brad remembers the strength of his father's grip and the gentleness of his mother's touch when he was fevered. He grew up talkative, attentive, and intelligent. His only hurts were scraped knees and jammed fingers. His world was perfect.

Until seventh grade. Something happened then. He began to have ideas of his own. His father, strong enough to create Brad's childhood world, was often too weak to accept a new thought. His strength, something Brad once saw as godlike, increasingly became a wall that prevented him from exploring new ideas.

Mostly, Brad feels, his father was trying to protect him. Later on, after Brad became an adult, he found out that his dad's younger brother had been killed by a car while they were riding bikes together. His dad had good reason to want to protect Brad.

There was also the hormone problem. When Brad was in sixth grade, he woke up one morning and discovered a curly hair in his pubic area. A week later there were several. Brad thought he might have some kind of disease. A friend told him he was stupid. That's the way it was with sexual discovery: Brad found out on his own, or from his friends. His parents never talked to him about sex, not even The Talk.

The closest his parents ever got to communicating to him about sex was the occasional muffled moans he would hear coming through their bedroom door. He discovered masturbation about the same time, found it exciting and interesting and retreated to the bathroom often. He soon was riddled with guilt, convinced for nearly a year that he would get a venereal disease, which he heard mentioned once on "Marcus Welby."

In Brad's mind a curious duality arose over his sexuality: pleasure and guilt, wonder and shame. He saw his first pinup girl at the age of thirteen, burning the image and the duality into his mind.

Adolescence was a difficult period for Brad. It marked not only his transition from child to adult, but his transition from a perfect world controlled by his father to an imperfect world controlled by his father. Brad's father allowed no room for deviance of thought or action. He had a plan for his son, one of safety, that demanded strict adherence. Without being consciously aware of it, and acting out of loving concern, Brad's father tried to control his son. He did not encourage Brad or often allow him to enter into the process of decision making.

The result was rebellion, mild at first. Brad's sexual experimentation was part curiosity, part peer pressure, part excitement, and part rebellion. He knew, even without his father talking to him about sex, that his dad wouldn't like what he was doing. Not one bit.

By the time he was a junior, he had been involved several times in heavy petting. Fortunately for Brad, most of the girls he went out with were "good" girls and drew the line at sexual intercourse. He lost his virginity, awkwardly, when he was a senior in high school. He thought he was in love, and, according to the wisdom of his high school world, people in love Do It. There was little pleasure in the experience for him or his girlfriend.

During college, in his newfound freedom, Brad increased his sexual activity. He had intercourse with a few more girls, most of whom he thought he loved. Except for one occasion, he avoided one-night stands. "I think I knew instinctively that sex was something much more than what my friends used to call 'jumping someone's bones,'" Brad says. "I knew it should never be that easy." There were also the occasional Playboys *and* Penthouses. *"I thought of pornography as easy, uninvolved," Brad says. "I thought that all it cost me was $2.75."*

Most of Brad's friends actually saw Brad as sexually conservative. He was not obsessed by sex, and he tried to be sensitive. Part of that he attributes to his upbringing. Although his parents made mistakes, he always knew he was loved. That was no small thing. He simply wasn't as needy as some of his more sexually active friends.

Another reason for his "restraint" was less tangible. "Although I was raised in a Christian home, my parents, by not talking about sex with me, never helped me make a connection between sex and God. But, deep in the recesses of my mind, I think I knew it anyway."

SEX IS FROM GOD AND IS A REFLECTION OF GOD

Even though Brad's dad did not handle well the sex education he gave his son, Brad stumbled onto a truth mentioned earlier: the connection between God and sex. God, the giver of all good things and the One who desires only the best for His children, created sex as one of His most wonderful gifts. Sex, in the wonderful light of Eden, must be understood in terms of the image of God. And the image of God, in turn, involves sexuality.

God specifically created humans as sexually distinct, male and female. Certain masculine aspects of His image He stamped onto the man; likewise, certain feminine aspects of His image He stamped onto the female. Through the act of sex, the image of God, in its masculine and feminine aspects, is completed.

Oneness, that mysterious biblical description of sex, is the blending of two people into a brilliant image of God.

SEX IS DESIGNED TO BE GIVEN, NOT RECEIVED

God designed sex as a way for one partner to give of himself or herself to another. This happens at many levels, from the giving of physical pleasure to the spiritual giving of the essence of oneself. Sex, at its best, is designed as a selfless expression of love.

This, of course, runs into the face of our culture's thinking. One always has to *get* something. Self-fulfillment, self-realization, self-love, and self-discovery are the buzzwords of our psychologists and soap opera stars. Most of the sexual promiscuity in our society can be directly related to selfish motivation. The reasoning goes something like this: I have unmet needs for pleasure, intimacy, and love, so I must get those needs taken care of.

Yet in reality, when it comes to sex, such self-seeking motivation will inevitably cause the person, as well as his or her partner, to self-destruct. Lacking in joy and purpose, sex entered selfishly can cause damage to self-esteem and identity. It is sex without context. It's like showing up for a basketball game in ice skates. It just doesn't work that way.

SEX LINKS THE PARTICIPANTS IRRETRIEVABLY

Sex is a lot of things to a lot of people—intimate, careless, kinky, obsessive, ecstatic, destructive, fulfilling. But what it isn't, and can never be, is casual. We must teach our children that God designed sex to be the fusing of one soul, through the body, to another soul, through the body. It is like bringing together the chemical elements sodium and chloride or hydrogen and oxygen. The result is an entirely new substance: salt or water.

The biblical concept of oneness is that, through the sex act, each participant irretrievably gives the other a part of his or her soul. Each person is thereby changed and an entirely new entity created, one that in God's design is never to be separated.

Sex works wonderfully in marriage. Two people give of the deepest parts of themselves, in the context of love and a lifelong commitment, and they are changed and united forever. They know, in a way like no other, deep union and intimacy. In such a context sex helps to build up and transform the two partners.

Cathy and John have never known each other. Their lives have never crossed. If you put them together at a party, they would not recognize each other. Yet, in some remarkable ways, they share a great deal.

Both Cathy's and John's respective fathers were dominating men. They seem to have come out of the same mold: alcoholic, verbally and sometimes physically abusive, and unable to show love with a touch.

Cathy's and John's childhoods, if they could be called childhoods, were dominated by the distance their respective fathers placed around themselves. Says Cathy, "I remember wanting to crawl up in my father's lap and just feel safe. He never let me do that." John's father was of German descent; both he and John's mother had immigrated to this country. He was determined and angry: "If he said something, and you didn't do it, you would likely end up on the ground."

Both Cathy and John were insecure and sickly. John had asthma so bad a special room had to be built for him to use from August until the first frost. He couldn't leave that room, which happened also to be his parent's bedroom. Cathy, often overwhelmed with feelings of loneliness, also spent hours in her room, which she used as a retreat to escape the turmoil of her home.

Both Cathy and John discovered, at a very early age, the power of their sexuality. Cathy cannot remember a time as a child when she didn't use masturbation to help her get to sleep at night. It helped blot out her parent's screaming. John remembers the first time he masturbated, at the age of twelve: "It became a drug for me almost overnight." He did it frequently: "It gave me a feeling of power. It was something I could escape to. I could build my own world." Both Cathy and John began creating fantasies of escape early in their childhoods.

Both were introverted. Cathy played the good girl: straight-A student, cheerleader, churchgoer, and member of all the right clubs. John was focused on pleasing people, even at the sacrifice of developing a personality. Cathy often took it upon herself to try to "rescue" her father. She would go to the bar after school and try to get him to come home and stop drinking. John's father died when he was thirteen.

Cathy's and John's sexual activity soon expanded. Although Cathy can't remember the details of her first sexual experience, she does remember her first long-term sexual relationship. She was fourteen; he was twenty. He was a college student from a well-connected family. She saw him as her ticket out. Sex, in her mind, was connected with power and money. Sex was her inroad: "The only way I could get attention and caring from a guy was to have sex."

She also enjoyed it: "I loved the feeling of power he had over me and I would do, and did, anything for him." Sex, she says, helped her to experience her "need and longing and the sick excitement that came with those feelings." They dated for four years, and he left her for college and then the army.

She also went to college—the only one of her family to do so. She wanted out. The first semester she slept with a "fair share" of men. Even though a nearly abusive situation at a party caused her to temporarily stop sleeping around, she began to mistake sex for love. "If a guy didn't want to have sex with me, that meant he didn't love me."

John was also very active sexually. The youngest of eleven children, he began exploring the body of one his sisters. No intercourse, but lots of fondling.

When he was fifteen, his family moved into a large house and rented the top floor out to college students. The college students took great joy in further introducing John to the pleasures of sex. They let him look through binoculars at the sorority house next door. They also introduced him to pornography. He still remembers, in great detail, his first Playboy centerfold: "It was burned into my mind. She was blonde; she was standing in front of a mirror with a plant in front of her, covering the lower half of her body, and a red robe or scarf draped over one shoulder. She was bare-breasted, and petite. That image was lodged in my mind as the ideal woman."

His fantasy life soon exploded. He would masturbate to photos of high school classmates. He went to great lengths to acquire pornography. Real sex could never measure up. The first time he had intercourse, he got gonorrhea. But that didn't stop him. If he could just have intercourse with his ideal woman, everything would be perfect. With each sexual disappointment, he would renew his commitment to find her. "The more sex I had, the more I wanted." The reality could never meet the expectation of his fantasy. With each frustration, came a new resolve to look a little harder.

CONVEY THE NEGATIVE CONSEQUENCES OF SEX OUTSIDE OF MARRIAGE

Rules must be connected to consequences, good and bad. Unfortunately, during adolescence our children can only "connect with" the negative consequences of sexual sin. Not until marriage will they be able to appreciate the positive consequences of sexual purity. This puts parents in the difficult position of having to deal with an extremely sensitive issue from a clearly negative perspective.

But that does not necessarily mean that we should start with the negative. We should start with the positive—that sex was designed as a wonderful gift. Once we have done that, the negatives can make sense and the rules do what they are designed to do: maximize the potential for the positive and eliminate the potential for the negative.

With that in mind, let's examine some of the negative consequences of sex outside the covenant of marriage.

SEX OUTSIDE MARRIAGE CAN OVERWHELM THE RELATIONSHIP

It has been said that when we "fall madly in love" about 25 percent of our brain is automatically disabled. When falling into love leads to falling into bed, the other 75 percent is sure to follow. Sex is not like playing cards. When you are dealing with the power of sex, it is increasingly difficult to stay in control of the game. Because of its powerful capacity to bond, and its intricate, multidimensional levels of intimacy, sex will almost always overwhelm the early stages of a relationship.

73

When you take the sexual restrictions off a relationship, you sacrifice the opportunity to get to know one another. Imagine telling two sixteen-year-olds it is OK to enjoy whatever level of sexuality they want, as long as it is "safe." Do you think they are going to spend two hours talking at a restaurant? Or go miniature golfing? No. They are going to find a secluded place and have sex. It is high-octane stuff. The results are twofold: the emotions released from the soul-to-soul bonding will overwhelm the relationship; and the skills necessary for a long-term relationship will be sacrificed.

Sexuality is designed to be an expression of love, not love itself. As such, it is meant to follow the process of knowing, and then loving, another person at deep levels of heart, mind, and soul.

The couple will confuse electricity for love. As long as they feel this good, what else could possibly be necessary? Entranced by their physical pleasures, they will not devote the time, energy, and discipline necessary to develop an infrastructure of skills that make a long-term relationship possible.

Learning to communicate, handle conflict, share dreams, understand compatibility, express past hurts, and know God requires a good deal of work and talk. Why go through that painful and tedious process when chills and thrills are available with a turn of a sheet? The preoccupation with sex in courtship usually leads to this question in marriage: Who are you?

Sexuality is designed to be an expression of love, not love itself. As such, it is meant to follow the process of knowing, and then loving, another person at deep levels of heart, mind, and soul. The infrastructure of a relationship—the exercise of skills and disciplines to truly know someone—must be built first. If love follows, then, in the lifelong commitment of marriage, sexuality can be a deep expression of a love slowly and tenderly crafted.

SEX OUTSIDE MARRIAGE
DISCONNECTS A PERSON FROM HIMSELF

In psychological terms, this phenomenon is known as shame, alienation, and fragmentation. It is impossible to walk away from sex unchanged, for sex is, by definition, the giving of the essence of oneself to another person. In sex outside marriage, you leave part of yourself with that sexual partner. You no longer feel whole. The seed of self-hatred can often take root. Oneness has happened on a deep level, and the stripping of the one back into two always leaves damage to the soul. A person becomes disconnected, in a very real sense, from himself or herself. One becomes a stranger to one's self.

SEX OUTSIDE MARRIAGE
DISCONNECTS A PERSON FROM GOD

In theological terms, this is known as guilt. And sin, as we know, separates a person from God. But sexual sin has an incalculable power to make people feel alone, stained, and incapable of connecting with God. Their sin, they feel, is just too great. They feel dirty. In fact, a deep part of themselves—their essence or identity—has been damaged.

For Christians, the guilt of falling to sexual sin is often overwhelming. I believe this is so because of the power of sex. Because sex is designed for intimate communication on several different levels, its abuse will result in across-the-board damage. One feels the devastation in mind, body, and soul.

SEX OUTSIDE MARRIAGE
DISCONNECTS A PERSON FROM HIS FUTURE SPOUSE

Time and again, I have counseled with couples whose story goes something like this. Female: "I don't feel I'm connecting with my spouse in sexual intercourse. It feels like only a fraction of him is present." Male: "I just can't seem to get my former sexual encounters out of my mind." If we are to understand the biblical concept of sexuality as being the irretrievable fusion of one soul into another, what is occurring in the couples' experience is not surprising: it is reasonable to assume that past sexual behavior will come back to haunt the very relationship it was designed to enhance.

SEX OUTSIDE MARRIAGE
WARPS GOD-GIVEN DESIRES

When sex occurs outside of God's design, it is always reduced. When we buy into such a reduction, we often risk trading love for lust, a longing for intimacy for an obsession with pleasure, and a lifelong fulfillment for a series of thrills. As we shall see, the reduction of sex also leads to the distortion of values. Pornography, addiction, perversion, and abuse are natural outcomes of disconnected sex. The probability for such distortions are almost guaranteed when a person brings into the equation a list of unmet needs and powerful drives. Disconnected sex, retaining its power but losing its purpose, can easily become a beast of enormous proportions, devouring people with obsession and addiction. The damage, even under the best of circumstances, may take a lifetime to repair.

REMEMBER THAT GOD GIVES GRACE

There is one other thing that we, as parents, must remember: God's grace. We must both claim it for ourselves and offer it to our children. We must claim it for ourselves because we are imperfect parents. Much of the damage done to our kids we ourselves do as parents. We must identify and repent of our sin, and continually seek God's wisdom and guidance. But even so, we will, in some ways, fail. We will, to varying degrees, inflict the consequences of our sin on our children. Some of us may painfully watch as the wounds we inflict push our children into sexual sin, and we may desperately need the forgiving, restoring touch of God's grace.

For the same reason, we must extend grace to our children. They will, no matter how well we teach them, also fail. Some will fall to sexual sin. Some will suffer grievous consequences. Most parents, I have discovered, can graciously handle any sins of their children but sexual sin. They apparently deem a sexual fall the unforgivable sin. But it isn't.

I'll never forget the day I met with a single woman and her seventeen-year-old daughter, who had just learned she was pregnant. What lingers in my mind was the tender way the mother stroked her daughter's shoulder and neck while her daughter confessed her sexual sin and its consequences. After the daughter's twenty-minute tear-filled explanation of her moral failure, the mother pulled her into a passionate embrace and kept repeating the simple phrase, "Please believe me that I still love you!" Moments later I added, "So do I, and more important, so does God!"

We parents must not create an extrabiblical category for sexual sin and convey the false notion that the promise of cleansing pertains to foul-ups of all kinds except sexual sins. No matter how devastating the situation seems, it is not the end of the world. God's grace is still available. And He wants to use us as conduits through which He can channel that grace to our kids and lovingly enter their moments of deepest crisis.

When Janine was growing up, she thought that life treated her pretty well. She was the good kid. She was on the honor roll. She had a lot of friends. She was everyone's favorite kid.

Including her father's. Her dad was, in many ways, impressive. He was brilliant, charismatic, and creative. He was an artist, a pilot, and could sing well. He changed jobs often, exercising new gifts or relieving boredom. His talents spanned the board: from devising ads for the yellow pages to designing and building his own home, start to finish.

But Janine's dad also had some terribly destructive quirks. He was controlling. His world had to be of his own creation. Everyone in his world had to be his puppet. He used his anger to manipulate. He beat his wife. Frequently. He beat her so much that the four children, at a young age, learned the procedure: run to the neighbors, call the police, and have Dad thrown in jail. The next day, repeat the same procedure. Janine's mom was beaten into submission. She made constant excuses for him. She had to take him back.

Janine was terrified of her father. She remembers the goodnight ritual they had in her house. The children had to kiss their parents before they went to bed. Janine would always kiss her dad first, quickly, and rush to her mom "so her kiss would wipe away his." But her dad, despite his "quirks," told Janine that he loved her. She was a child, and children were supposed to believe their parents.

When she was in the seventh grade, her parents divorced. Five months later, Janine's dad came for a late night visit. She was in bed and heard her mom scream: nothing unusual, she always heard her mom scream. But, this time, she knew it was different. While looking for a place to hide, she heard the police pull up and talk to her father through a bullhorn. Janine decided to make a run for it. As she ran past her dad in the kitchen, she saw blood spurting from both of his wrists.

She later learned that her father had stabbed her mother with a hunting knife. Nearly killed her. Then he tried to kill himself. Later, as the police questioned her, Janine remembers laughing. It was the only thing left to do.

In her childhood, Janine was competent. She had a remarkable ability to focus her attention and accomplish nearly anything. When she was seventeen, she was named Junior Miss. But behind the competency, almost subconsciously, Janine felt there was something wrong. Part of it was the drug and alcohol abuse, the frequent quest to be numb. Part of it was that she had a lot of friends but no real communication. Another part, perhaps even more disturbing, was her attitude about sex. There was, at the same time, a sense of power and powerlessness about it.

She first heard about intercourse from her brother. She was in fifth grade and thought it was gruesome. Maturing quickly, growing to her full height at the age of twelve, she hung around the older boys. She often found herself being attracted to people who wanted to use her. Janine had no moral code. How could she have, with her parents? Her only guiding principle was this: do whatever you want, just don't let Mom find out.

Without any sense of right or wrong, Janine thought of sex as just one more area in which she could prove competent. She viewed her body as a tool. "Sex was like insurance," she says. "Sex was just another thing to do to get someone to like me. Sex was to be expected, not really a choice." She had lots of sexual encounters, flirting and heavy petting, but only three relationships that involved intercourse. She wanted to be a good girl and sexy at the same time.

Her mom remarried when she was in ninth grade and began confiding in Janine about her new sex life, about how much better it was than before. Janine felt violated, almost creepy.

It was at about the same time that she heard about the transforming power of the gospel. She went to visit her older sister, a Christian, in Florida. She was attracted to God, partly because of a nagging sense of emptiness. She accepted Christ, was baptized in the Atlantic, and, when she couldn't sustain the "high," quickly discarded her newfound faith. It was a pattern that was to continue—committing and discarding—until her first year in college, when she finally began to understand what it meant to make Jesus Lord of her life.

She then became a competent Christian.

Sadly, Janine's story does not move from conversion to a "happy ever after" conclusion, as we shall see in a later chapter. As in so many other cases, sins committed behind the doors of her childhood home haunted her well into her adult years. Sexual sin can never be taken lightly.

CHAPTER 4

PASSION

For a week or two, it was to be a sexual paradise. That's the way we had it pictured. Florida, the hot sun, the beach, and, best of all, the bedroom. Pure ecstasy. After a victorious and difficult struggle to remain sexually pure before our marriage, Lynne and I were finally going to get what we deserved. Sex. And plenty of it. That was before some cosmic sense of humor kicked in. Our honeymoon was a disaster. We could easily write a book of memoirs, *We Flopped in Florida.*

First came the sunburns. Severe ones. The kind that bring nausea, then blistering and peeling. Our cries of "I want you, I have to have you!" turned into "Don't you dare touch me!" While we were recovering from our sunburns, Lynne developed a cold sore. Not just an average cold sore, mind you: it stretched from her lip to the middle of her neck. I am exaggerating a little, but not much. I laughed about it. Lynne, not surprisingly, accused me of being insensitive and didn't exactly feel like Cindy Crawford. That was our sexual debut.

The early years of our marriage didn't exactly scorch the planet either. Due to our ignorance and circumstances, we did just about everything possible to eliminate sexual fulfillment. I was a full-time youth minister and a full-time college student. We had two boarders and their dogs living with us in a two-bedroom, cracker-box house. Lynne had two full-term pregnancies, during which she was sick four to five times a day for nine months, and two pregnancies that ended in miscarriages, during which she was just as sick. Add to that the all-too-common inability to communicate about sex, and you get the idea. When we were hot, it was often in anger, not passion. We lived like this for years.

On our eighth wedding anniversary, I wanted to make up everything to Lynne. We would finally get to be the sexual dynamos we knew we really were. With the help of a friend, who was the manager of a hotel, I planned an elaborate anniversary celebration. A veritable sexual feast.

At first, everything went according to plan. We had a romantic dinner together, and then, after checking into our hotel, we were awestruck with our room; it was the mother of all honeymoon suites: mirrors everywhere, a huge Jacuzzi and sauna, and, in the center of it all, a bed on a platform. For the next few hours, we enjoyed all the accoutrements. We watched a movie, lit the candles, and enjoyed the evening. And we were both confident that the best was yet to come. But time was slipping away; the midnight hour was approaching.

I decided to whisper something incredibly sensuous into my wife's ear, to plant a tender seed that would sprout into wild romance: "Honey, let's hit the sack," I blurted out. We blew out the candles, climbed into bed, and looked up at the mirrors. Just as I wrapped her in my arms, I heard her whisper, "The curtains aren't closed tightly enough."

It didn't matter to her that we were on the twenty-fifth floor. She said she wanted to sleep in, and the morning light would wake her. She got up. "Should I turn the light on?" I asked. "No," she said, and then I heard a strange noise, followed by a soft "Oh-oh." I turned the lights on. Lynne had walked into one of the four-cornered mirrors around the bedpost.

It took seven stitches to repair the damage to her forehead. Our passion was spent, not in a honeymoon suite but in the emergency room of a hospital.

Sexual dreams don't always become reality. Many people have unrealistic expectations about sex:

- Sex will bring joy, passion, and unending ecstasy to my life
- Sex will solve my problems or depression
- Sex will make me feel constantly bonded with my husband
- Sex will stop me from masturbating
- Sex will make life all seem like a fairy tale, complete with a happy ending

Let me tell you, sex is not the cure-all for our problems; moreover, it takes work, discipline, spiritual maturity, and honesty to provide the environment for our sexual competency to mature. We will often fail. Good sex, the kind that outlives infatuation and expresses oneness of souls, rarely comes easily. Most couples have the scars to prove it.

The early era in a marriage is critical. During those years, there is passion—the passion of sexual energy, the passion of conflict, and sometimes both at the same time. Through the storm of emotions, there must be reason, strategy, and discipline. Creating an environment of love, honesty, and security for one another means not allowing each other to be carried along on the wave of emotion that so often marks the first years of marriage. Carefully thought-through patterns of understanding and relating to one another must be discussed, implemented, and practiced. Otherwise, the passion, uncontrolled and undisciplined, may drown the marriage.

Rebecca married a man almost completely different from her father, who, as we have seen, dominated her childhood by creating a mystery and near-terror in her mind about sex.

On her wedding day, the contrast could not have been greater. Her father rarely opened up, especially about sex; her husband talked about things that could make you blush or gag. At the supper table.

Her father was legalistic and often lifeless; her husband was free and passionate. Her father was stiff-backed and stiff-lipped in church; her husband chattered and sometimes giggled in the back pew. Her father raised his children in a strict environment where love was implied, not expressed. Her husband was raised in a loose and slightly crazy world where expressions of love allowed for choice and risk. Her father would probably not even acknowledge the reality of an orgasm; her husband often referred to it as The Big O.

During their first year of marriage, their sex was phenomenal. That surprised Rebecca somewhat. They had made the mistake of occasionally having sexual intercourse during their dating relationship—perhaps ten times during the five months. During those times, she would often picture her dad in her mind; the quality of the sex depended on how strong that image was. Her fear kept them from having sex more often. That, in a way, was a blessing because they were able to keep sex from becoming the focus of their dating relationship. They got to know each other.

When they married, they were best friends. Because her father had told her that sex was permissible within marriage, the light in her mind turned from red to green. She went crazy with it. They had sex one or two times a day. They did the Wild Thing. Practically anywhere, anytime. Even though she never had orgasms, she found a certain amount of physical pleasure. It was one more way that she could get close to her husband. She just couldn't seem to get enough of him.

Gradually, her passion subsided. She started to realize that sex was, for her, little more than a physical act. Soon, when she started to come to grips with how her parents had failed her, she began to think she was using sex as a Band-aid to cover up deeper hurts. Her misgivings about sex were increased by two events, both of which occurred in the second year of their marriage: they had their first baby, and they became Christians.

The baby brought another person, another soul for Rebecca to love. That made her husband no longer as necessary for meeting her relational needs. Their Christianity, which contrasted dramatically with the empty religion they had both been raised with, was making them ask different questions. Should sex be something more? Are simultaneous orgasms the definition of good sex?

At first, the questions brought tension. Rebecca became more confused about sex. The mystery of the stapled pages came back to haunt her. Was there something about sex that should make her feel shame and embarrassment, like her mom? How could she feel intimacy when she had such nagging questions?

Rebecca dealt with her confusion through escape. She began to withdraw from sex. Her husband, however, did not share her lack of interest. He still wanted sex. He became demanding. And the more demanding her husband became, the more she would retreat.

In the next four years, Rebecca had three more children. During that time, their sex life remained strained, although they devoted a great deal of attention to developing their marriage and family. Her husband had a difficult time in not seeing sex as intercourse and orgasm. Rebecca often tried to redefine sex as him rubbing her back and giving her feet a massage. Her husband would say sure, and then, two minutes later, return to his own definition.

They fought about sex more than any other issue. But as bad as things got, they always felt a commitment to one another for the long haul. They knew no one was going to walk out on the other. That gave them the freedom of security. They didn't try to hide from one another in fear. When they were angry, they were angry. When one of them thought the other was being controlling, he or she would say so. They always tried to talk things through. Even in the heat of passion, they knew that if they did not communicate, they did not stand a chance.

Although they were young Christians, they knew as well there must be a least one other form of communication:

prayer. "We didn't know a lot of things about the Bible," Rebecca says. "But we knew we should talk to God."

Even though they did not know the theological reasons, Rebecca and her husband began to learn in church that without God their sexual frustration would continue and that good sex must begin with God. Without Him, they would have little hope for sexual fulfillment. There are at least two reasons that good sex begins with God, one defensive, the other, offensive.

PLACING GOD FIRST DEFENDS US AGAINST EVIL

The world, even a fool would tell you, is not a place given to sexual purity. We are told, in a thousand different ways through a dozen different mediums, to indulge our desires. "Stop fighting the urge; give in," the messages scream. Pleasure, instantaneous and immediately fulfilling, becomes the goal. And let's be honest: doesn't that sound wonderful? Aren't we all drawn to such a promise?

Sexual sin doesn't just happen. It almost always is the result of a process of nurturing temptation. When . . . people [with whom we feel a sexual chemistry] are placed in our lives . . . our natural inclination is to run from or nurture temptation. Both tacks will likely lead to sexual sin.

Seen in the light of this enticing promise, God's design for sex comes up short. Our culture relegates commitment, discipline, forgiveness, and perseverance to the bin labeled "Outdated and

Obsolete." We content ourselves with superficial understanding and pleasure while neglecting deeper realities. We spend much time in avoiding pain and indulging self-absorption. In relationships, more times than not, we skim the surface.

How are we to learn to love one another sexually when we can't even understand one another? How are we supposed to express love sexually when we are dealing with the damage of being raised in broken families? How are we to communicate tenderly with a kiss when we can't even say a word without anger? Why should we go to all the trouble of dealing with deep issues in our lives when there is instant pleasure available around the corner? We would love to give God's way a try—we really would—if we weren't already so exhausted.

Left to our own resources, more times than not, we will sin sexually. The pressures are just too great. That is why a vital relationship with God is critical. Without it, good sex is simply not possible. Only fully devoted, committed, authentic Christians can feel the inner tug of the Holy Spirit, the voice that tells us, "Abhor evil, cling to good." Only when we are focused on pleasing God and giving Him glory in all of our actions will we find the inner spiritual stamina and enthusiasm to pursue righteousness and purity. That is our only defense.

I think of Joseph. Listen to his story as recorded in Genesis 39:6–11:

> Now Joseph was well-built and handsome, and after a while his master's wife took notice of Joseph and said, "Come to bed with me!"

> But he refused. "With me in charge," he told her, "my master does not concern himself with anything in the house; everything he owns he has entrusted to my care. No one is greater in this house than I am. My master has withheld nothing from me except you, because you are his wife. How then could I do such a wicked thing and sin against God?" And though she spoke to Joseph day after day, he refused to go to bed with her or even be with her.

> One day he went into the house to attend to his duties, and none of the household servants was inside. She caught him by the cloak and said, "Come to bed with me!" But he left his cloak in her hand and ran out of the house.

Joseph was practically raped by a woman who was, in all likelihood, a beautiful woman. Blow the dust off of this story and put yourself in the place of Joseph. Can you imagine the force of the temptation? After all, no one would ever have to know. It could have been an hour of paradise.

What if, by way of comparison, a fashion model came to your home when your wife was away and started undressing you? Would you be able to resist? What would stop you? Clearly, Joseph's temptation is not just a dry story; the hormones practically leap off the page.

One key thought kept Joseph from indulging. "How then could I do such a wicked thing and sin against God?" Joseph knew that going to bed with this woman would be more than a roll in perfumed linens. It would violate his relationship with God. Joseph's love for and fear of God defended him against the power of naked sexual aggression. Such power can only be attributed to the supernatural protection of God.

Through his commitment to God, Joseph was able to escape the temptation. His decision to honor God, however, was not an on-the-spot decision. Earlier, and all along the way, he made willful decisions to refuse to nurture temptation. He did not just run from temptation, he attacked it. Through a steely resolve to God, he refused to let his mind wander on lustful thoughts, although he had plenty of opportunities to do so.

Sexual sin doesn't just happen. It almost always is the result of a process of nurturing temptation. When attractive people are placed in our lives, people with whom we feel a sexual chemistry, our natural inclination is to run from or nurture temptation. Both tacks will likely lead to sexual sin.

If we run, we will fail to deal with the real problem: how to deal with sexual sin. Wherever we run, even if it is to a distant state, we will someday be faced with the same sexual dilemma.

If we nurture temptation—slowly creating fantasies in our mind of candlelight dinners, romance, and, finally, sexual encounters, we will allow the seed of lust to take root in the heart, which, in turn, will set off a cycle of sin.

The cycle is described in James 1:14–15: "Each one of us is tempted when, by his own evil desire, he is dragged away and enticed. Then, after desire has conceived, it gives birth to sin; and sin, when it is full-grown, gives birth to death." I believe this is part of what Jesus was saying in His statement "Anyone who looks at a woman lustfully has already committed adultery with her in his heart." Adultery is not a one-time act; it begins when a person nurtures temptation in the heart.

We are especially prone to nurture sexual temptation during periods of conflict, disillusionment, and stress, either inside or outside the marriage. We crave relief from the pressure. In such a mental climate, nurturing sexual temptation often begins with an "innocent" fantasy. What would it be like to have a new life? What would it be like to have a new spouse? What would it be like to go to bed with that person? As the questions escalate, the fantasy moves steadily from the ethereal to the physical—and toward reality. When such nurturing occurs for long periods of time, it is only a matter of time before adultery happens in the flesh.

When Joseph faced temptation, he did not seek to run from his job, nor did he nurture lustful thoughts. Well before the offer to go to bed, Joseph had developed and clarified his values. He knew what he would do and wouldn't do and why. The theme of his life had already been clearly articulated and engraved on his heart: "I will honor God." When the moment of the worst temptation actually came, he didn't have to weigh the options. He was able to say immediately: "How then could I do such a wicked thing and sin against God?"

I am not saying that we should put ourselves at risk by needlessly placing ourselves in situations where sexual temptation may occur. Whenever possible, it is critical to take measures to stay away from situations that could prove to be sexually tempting. In my own life, I have established a set of guidelines that include:

- avoiding meals alone in restaurants with women other than my wife
- avoiding riding alone with a woman in a car
- avoiding meeting alone with a woman in my office (unless my assistant is right outside my glass-paneled door)

Given the power of sexual temptation, it is pure foolishness not to take preventative measures. Yet, at the same time, we must be aware that, no matter how many preventative measures we take, sexual temptation will find us. The question then becomes: how do we handle it? If our value system has not been clearly established beforehand, as was Joseph's, we will be in trouble. The best defense is a predetermined and heartfelt commitment to honoring God. When that is one's heart condition, it frees one to understand and negotiate the feelings of sexual temptation when they inevitably come.

PLACING GOD FIRST TEACHES US HOW TO LOVE

Building a good defense is not the only reason God is vital to sexual fulfillment. Good sex goes much deeper than avoiding bad sex. Here again we see the fundamental principle about sex couples need to remember: that good sex involves a deep connection with another in love, self-giving, respect, acceptance, and oneness, and if we are not in an intimate and authentic relationship with God, we will never learn the skills necessary for good sex.

How can you love your wife if you do not understand and experience what God's love is? How can you give yourself to another without letting the reality of a God who died on a cross penetrate your heart? How can you know what it means to be one with another if you do not understand the passion of Jesus for unity with His people?

We learn love, self-giving, and intimacy through a relationship with Jesus Christ. The better we know Him through an open heart and renewed mind, the better we are able to develop our sexuality within the fabric of God's design. If we are not connected to God, we are forced to rely on ourselves—we who are sinful and given to manipulation, self-seeking, and self-destruction. Left to our own devices, we are as likely to experience good sex as an artist is to create an ice sculpture with a blow torch.

God wants to transform every aspect of our lives. The movement He desires is always the same: from self-seeking to self-giving. That is particularly true of our sexuality. He wants us each to use the gift that He has given to meet the needs of another, not out of a sense of obligation or duty but out of love.

When sex works properly in marriage, both partners give of themselves entirely, and, as a result, both partners enjoy. Such giving and receiving is inherently difficult work. Just as the compass points north, the automatic human tendency is toward selfish interests. Without the transforming power of God and His Word, we are incapable of escaping our own selfish desires.

After high school, Brad left God. Maybe he mistook God the Father for his father. It was his father, you remember, who created the paradox of his childhood: the safety and joy of his early years, and the overprotection of his life as a teenager. As he grew into an adult, Brad looked at Christianity as oppressive—a set of rules that never allowed him to exercise personal initiative or acknowledged his personal opinions and perspective. He felt as though he were being forced into a mold. Maybe it was that he needed to discover his own reality. His faith was always his parents' faith; it seldom cut an edge in his own heart. Maybe it was rebellion. He had grown fond of sin.

He ignored God. Sometimes that worked; sometimes not. Sexually, it was not difficult. He believed that God had little to say about sex, except no. No one had taught him that God's design for sex was overwhelmingly positive, and, without that potential reward to guide him, he pursued his own vision for sexuality.

But he never bought into the concept of casual sex. His early childhood, those years of deep joy, had taught him the importance of love. Sex, he knew, must be in the context of caring relationships. He sought to be careful.

He dated frequently and never pursued sex until there was a level of trust, openness, and love. Or what he thought was love. He had sex in three different relationships. "Sex," he says, "was just one way to express love to another person. I really felt that it was OK, a very positive thing." A near-suicide changed his mind. He had dated a girl for about six months, and they had sex ten or twelve times. They both thought they loved one another, although there was never any mention of future commitment. "We had intense feelings for one another on a lot of different levels."

And then the feelings wore off. For him, at least. "I don't know how to explain it," Brad says. "I know what we had was real, but I just couldn't see spending the rest of my life with her." The day after he broke it off, she took a bottle full of sleeping pills. "She called me in the middle of the night, and her voice was slurred and slow. She just kept saying the same thing over and over, 'I gave myself to you, I gave myself to you, I gave myself to you.'"

He can still hear the echo in his head.

After that, Brad bounced from one relationship to another. They never lasted longer than three months. He had sex occasionally but, contrary to his earlier pattern, only when he barely knew the girl. "I was operating out of fear," he says. "I didn't want to hurt anyone again, so I thought I could reduce sex to something equivalent to playing Monopoly. If it was only a game, designed only for pleasure, no one would get hurt." In looking back, he can see that the girls he had sex with were "kind of emotional zombies." They seemed numb to everything in life, except pleasure. They were one-dimensional and mostly sad. "Almost disconnected from themselves," he says.

Brad could relate to that. Increasingly during the next few years, he felt like a stranger to himself. Generally carefree, he began to wrestle with bouts of anxiety and depression. As much as he tried to keep God out of the picture, he began to experience "gnawing, bizarre" pangs of guilt. He began to realize that his craving for independence, free from dogma (both his father's and his Father's), had cost him. He had made decisions, often tinged with rebellion, just for the sake of making decisions.

His independence had become a god. He had thought that his sexuality was one of the best ways to assert his independence and, at the same time, show love. Slowly he began to realize that self-centered independence and love do not go together. "The reason the sex was so deadly," he says, "is that I was using it as a tool to meet my needs." He understood, at the very least, that self-gratification should never be an end in itself.

As his relationships became more superficial and he witnessed the splintering in his life and the slow drain of purpose, he began to return to God for healing. He was twenty-eight and alone. "Love and sex had left me with fear," he says. "I knew there had to be something more." Six months after committing his life to God, he met a young woman in church. As they devoted their energies to the church together, they felt an instant bonding. They thought it was love. At the strong urging of their parents and friends (he was, after all, getting older), they announced their engagement.

About the same time, after hearing a message on seeking forgiveness, Brad decided to call his old girlfriend: the one who had tried to commit suicide. He wanted to tell her he was sorry and seek forgiveness for the hurt that he had caused her. When he could not find her name in the telephone book, he decided to call her parents. Their daughter, the mother said coolly, had committed suicide a few months ago. She had had another broken love affair.

The difference between love and lust is one mark of the disparity between the world's design for sex and God's design. Lust, through its filter of selfishness, warps natural, God-given desires. Admiring the grace and beauty of a woman as a unique and wonderful creation of God, when filtered through lust, reduces the woman to an object. She ceases to be an image-bearer of God and becomes merely a thing capable of fulfilling selfish needs.

That is why pornography is so dangerous. In its milder forms, women become mindless, soulless bodies of flesh. Pornographic magazines portray sexual gratification as the woman's desire. In pornography's more wicked forms, women are reduced to sex objects. The pornographic philosophy goes something like this. *Sex is simply the right of men. Women, even when they are raped, love it. The only purpose of women is to meet the selfish sexual interests of men. Lust is all that matters.* Lust reduces the wonder, intricacy and beauty of a whole person to an object that can be used for one purpose: sexual pleasure.

As we have seen, Jesus shocked His listeners by equating lust with adultery. His words are even more shocking when read in their context. Matthew 5:27–30 states:

> You have heard that it was said, "Do not commit adultery." But I tell you that anyone who looks at a woman lustfully has already committed adultery with her in his heart. If your right eye causes you to sin, gouge it out and throw it away. It is better for you to lose one part of your body than for your whole body to be thrown into hell. And if your right hand causes you to sin, cut it off and throw it away. It is better for you to lose one part of your body than for your whole body to go into hell.

Jesus' words went far beyond the law and struck at religious, external notions of righteousness. For the Pharisees, keeping the law was all that mattered. For Jesus, righteousness was a matter of internal realities—the condition of the heart. What Jesus was saying was this: lust always involves the reduction of another person. The object of the lust, in the heart of the one who is lusting, becomes less than fully human. Adultery is no more than the outworking of that reductionism.

God has stamped His image on each human. He does not take kindly to any thought or action that causes one of His image bearers to be reduced and used. That is why Jesus' language is so strong. In the cosmic scheme of things, it would be better to cut off your hand or gouge out your eye than to so blatantly smear the image of God.

The language of amputation—the cutting off of a hand or the gouging out of an eye—is no accident. Since the act of lust results in the severe fragmentation of a person from human to object, it would, in fact, be better to have individual body parts severed than to reduce another in such a debilitating fashion. That would be a preferable form of amputation.

In almost every case I can think of, sexual sin involves the act of lust, the movement of reductionism. As we have seen, it is certainly true of pornography. Jesus said it was true of adultery. But what about other sexual sins—abuse, fornication, addiction, fantasy? The same is true of them. When the sex drive is out of control, the God-given design of sexuality is reduced for selfish motivation.

Self-gratification short-circuits God's design for sex and, as with all efforts motivated by selfishness, will eventually end in self-destruction. Sin kills. Pornography leads to chauvinistic and perverted attitudes about women and eventually kills the wonder and beauty of making love to a whole person. Adultery violates trust and love, and rips a hole in the heart of at least three people. Sexual abuse feeds an evil sickness in the perpetrator and creates a rage deeper than the pit of hell in the victim. In every case, the deep-rooted needs that drove the selfish behaviors not only remain unmet but gain a stronger hold. Through reductionism, sex becomes an issue of control, power, and domination. That's why, so many times, sexual sin ends in addiction, neurosis, psychosis, and obsession.

> *The childhood worlds of John and Cathy, which we discovered in the previous chapter were disconnected from intimacy and love, helped to create a vicious cycle in their lives: endless sexual hunger and endless disappointment.*
>
> *As they entered into their respective marriages, John and Cathy hoped that marriage would end their struggle with sexual temptation. John married his high school sweetheart. Cathy married the first man who showed tenderness to her.*
>
> *Two years before his marriage, John had gotten his future wife pregnant. John's request to marry her at that time was refused by her parents because she was only seventeen. The baby was put up for adoption. Now, two years later, they were old enough.*
>
> *The man Cathy married treated her like a queen. A solid Christian, he told her that he wanted to save sex for marriage. That relieved and disappointed Cathy. Although she was tired of the pain of her sexual experimentation, she also felt rejected. Says Cathy, "I felt that if he didn't want me sexually, I could not feel loved." That feeling brought more guilt.*
>
> *Cathy and John both hoped that their needs would be met through marriage. They hoped to find the love, touch, and tenderness they missed as children. They hoped marriage would help them to stop equating sexual hunger with love. Each hoped to be happily married. They were wrong.*

Actually, both knew before their respective marriages began that they didn't stand a chance. The clues were obvious.
John continued to have sex with other women, before and
after his marriage. He hardly stopped to take a breath to say
"I do." He was simply living out the mind-set, straight from
the Penthouse Forum, that, when it came to sex, the more
partners the better. That was just the way life was to be lived.
Cathy, shortly before her marriage, had sex with a former
boyfriend. Her explanation, "It was sort of like a binge before
a diet," she says.

Marital sex did not fulfill either John or Cathy. Neither
had found his or her ideal lover. For John, that lover was the
first Playboy centerfold he saw as a boy; for Cathy, the lover
could be any man of power and prestige.

Both became addicted, but in different directions. John
had his sex on the road. After serving time in Vietnam, he
became a traveling salesman. There, he found "a lot of lonely
people looking for companionship." Sex made it seem less
lonely. His life was a blur of activity: the pursuit of money,
parties, pleasure, and sex. He did not stop long enough to
look inside; he was afraid of the darkness. He was a professional liar and lied to his wife, his boss, and himself. He
sacrificed everything in pursuit of a good time.

Cathy also escaped sexually. Her husband, she felt, "didn't
seem to need sex to fulfill him." For Cathy, sex was synonymous with love and, therefore, essential. Her husband was
drafted shortly after their marriage. A few months later,
Cathy got a call to come visit her husband at the base. After a
five-hundred-mile drive, she stopped at a Holiday Inn and
called her husband. He would not be able to leave the base
until the next day.

Cathy was upset and cried. The desk clerk at the hotel offered her comfort; they ended up in bed together. The next
night she slept with her husband. A few weeks later, she
found out that she was pregnant. She didn't tell her husband
that the child might not be his. A few years later, feeling "un-
wanted and unnoticed" by a busy husband, she had sex with
her best friend's husband. "It was exciting to feel wanted,"
Cathy says. "Exciting, but not fulfilling." What she really

wanted, she says, was for her husband to want her sexually, passionately. It was, essentially, a question of control. Yet, at the same time, she wanted to feel overwhelmed by him.

The pain and fear of her affairs drove her away from actual physical affairs. In a technical sense, she never cheated on her husband again. She did, however, withdraw into her own private world of fantasy. In such a world, she believed, her "lovers" were always perfect, powerful, and safe.

John, on the other hand, had no such fantasies. He attempted to control his wife, a gentle and loving woman. He lied to her. He belittled her. He tried to make her feel stupid and overweight. Certainly not the perfect woman. Not by a long shot.

He didn't tell her about the affairs. That was his business; he deserved them. Then one day, under his intense questioning, his wife admitted that she herself had had an affair while he was in Vietnam. Worse, it was with a friend of his. He said he understood, but on the inside he was destroyed. He did not comprehend, even remotely, his violation of a double standard.

Cathy and John's behavior illustrates the outworking of a consequence of the scientific worldview mentioned earlier in this book: devotion to the extremes of fear and lust. When people fall into sexual sin and experience its disappointment and pain, they are likely to attempt to dampen their pain in one or both of those self-protective strategies. Sometimes they give themselves over to abandonment, or lust, the pursuit of sexual pleasure. Although they know quickly in their journey that sexuality can never do what they want it to—fill the hole in their souls—they continue to pursue it. And they continue to be disappointed, hurt, and disconnected. Subconsciously or consciously, they make a decision to pursue pleasure at any cost.

To do this, they must quell their guilt, their longing for something more, and any concern they may have for the legitimate needs of others. In this style of relating, people pursue pleasure and relief at the sacrifice of values; this forces them to shut down conscience, soul, and spirit.

Moving toward the opposite extreme, fear, or isolation, has a similar effect. Having been hurt by sexuality, they fear it. They separate themselves, vow never to be hurt and vulnerable in the future, construct massive walls, and are never as open again. They view sex as painful and humiliating, even in the context of marriage. They do their duty, if they have to. Often, their longings redirect themselves with impressive energy into competency, fantasy, and perfectionism. Control is the key element. And control often leads to loneliness and contempt. Their commitment to isolation results in not loving or being loved and having lots of surface relationships.

Whether people pursue abandonment or isolation, they are tampering with legitimate longings for something more. They are agreeing to settle for less. That's what sin does: it reduces our humanity. Instead of pursuing love, which has to do with self-giving, they pursue lust, which has to do with self-expansion. They lust after pleasure—sex without the danger of commitment, or they lust after separation—sex without the danger of intimacy.

But those who sin sexually hurt more than themselves. They hurt their partners. Let's say a husband has learned a pattern of pleasure without intimacy. By focusing on himself, he has learned how to shut down a part of himself. His wife, of course, feels uncared for and disconnected. Those feelings often lead her into sin by seeking other sources of fulfillment, which leads to more pain, hurt, and disappointment, which in turn leads to more shutting down.

Unchecked sin leads to more sin. The destructive cycle expands. You can't shut down the longing of a soul. If that longing is not met in God, it will resurrect itself in any number of ways: shame, guilt, anger, rebellion, depression—and, of course, more sin: trying to order the world through selfishness.

When sexual sin is confined to the context of marriage and commitment, the damage will be more limited. But if sex is pursued outside the context of marriage, in a world without rules and boundaries, the potential for harm is almost beyond belief. When sex is not founded upon giving oneself away in unending love, almost anything can happen. Anything evil.

In her childhood, Janine lived under the illusion that her world was pretty much OK. She was, after all, a Junior Miss, a good student, a popular girl. Sure, there were faults in her childhood. Her dad was abusive and controlling; she tended to use a few too many drugs and drink a little too much; and she had a perplexing view of sex as both dirty and powerful. But then again, no child's world was perfect. The problems weren't anything that a little bit of competency couldn't fix. And Janine, as we have seen, prided herself on her competency. For the most part, she considered herself lucky.

The first flashback shattered her dream world. It came nine years into her marriage while she was driving her car. The images in her mind were of white sheets, a chenille bedspread, and sun streaming through the windows. There was a small body next to a huge, hairy body. Things were being touched that were not supposed to be touched. The flash lasted only a few seconds.

Within a few months, Janine was hospitalized, suicidal, and losing hold of reality. Her childhood—the real one that is—was coming back to haunt her. The repressed memories, in wave after wave of terrifying flashbacks, revealed that she was a victim of sexual abuse. By her father, grandmother, stepfather, and other assorted evil people.

Janine's life, the one occupied by a former Junior Miss and a good wife and mother, had been exposed as a lie. The memories of abuse overwhelmed her. They violently contradicted the life she had made for herself. She had escaped some abusive relationships to marry a godly, caring Christian man. They had adequate sex. They had good children. Janine was involved in ministry; she faithfully had devotions and prayed the way she was supposed to. She was a very good Christian girl. Everything was under control.

Or so she thought. Even before the flashbacks began, she had begun to feel empty, disconnected, and joyless. She had plenty of friends but little intimacy. Her life seemed superficial. "I prayed, God answered, and my life was changing. It just wasn't real deep. It was as deep as I would let it go." Janine avoided the extremes, trying to steer a middle course in her relationships, emotions, and life. She tried to keep a rein on things. She was living flat and safe.

And then came the flashbacks. Control was no longer possible. She was immersed into a sea of terror, shame, and fear. Each new wave of memories revealed deeper and deeper levels of depravity in her abusers.

The abuse had begun early. When she was five, a kindergartner, she remembers masturbating her father. About the same time, her grandmother used to attack her sexually with a Barbie doll and then make her play with the doll. In the next few years until her parents were divorced when she was in seventh grade, she was raped repeatedly by her uncle and her father.

But that wasn't the worst of it. She began having memories of ritualistic, satanic abuse by the members of a cult when she was only six or seven. They would rape her, and abuse her verbally. Once they put her in a coffin and told her they were going to kill her. During another attack they gave her a shot that knocked her out. When she woke up, they told her that Janine was dead and that she had turned into an animal. "You look like Janine and sound like Janine," they told her, "but you are really an animal, because we killed Janine."

Janine, in fact, had not died. She had escaped. In her mind, while the abuse was occurring, she imagined herself flying away on the back of a warm, tender creature with thick white fur and silver wings. To a beach, maybe. Where she was the princess of the sand castle she was making. It was there that she was able to forget. Says Janine, "God gave me the ability to dissociate, so that I could 'be' someplace else while the abuse was going on. I tucked away the abuse itself in some part of my mind and locked it up tight."

The process of dissociation is not unusual in children who are sexually abused. It is as though the mind knows that the child cannot handle the abuse and allows it to be stored away until she is better able to deal with it, usually well into adult life. The child is able to go on with life. Often, when the abuse is severe, the personality will split. The pressure is simply too great.

100

For Janine, the sexual abuse was physically horrendous. But that was nothing compared to the damage to her emotions and soul. She had been controlled and used by the people who were supposed to love and nurture her.

When the first wave of memories began, Janine stopped functioning. She thought she was going crazy. She was terrified that her father would show up and kill her. (After each abuse, her father would tell her that if she ever told anyone, he would kill her and her mother.) She became suicidal. For four months, she hardly ate. She couldn't sleep. She was on four or five different medications—antidepressants, antipsychotics, tranquilizers, sleeping pills.

Worst of all, Janine lost hold of the reality of God. Two of her flashbacks particularly devastated her. In the first one, little Janine was strapped to a table, and she heard the sounds of a calf (which was to be sacrificed to Satan). She began to sing to herself, "Away in a manger, no crib for a bed, the little Lord Jesus lay down His sweet head. . . . The cattle are lowing, the poor baby wakes. But little Lord Jesus, no crying He makes." She prayed, as fervently as a six-year-old can, for Jesus to stay by her side. In the second flashback, the situation was similar: Janine on a bed being raped by her father. As Janine looked around the room to find Jesus, she imagined that she saw Him. In a dark corner. With His hands in His pockets.

RESTORING PASSION TO YOUR MARRIAGE

When we hear such stories we are outraged. *Thank God I am not a child abuser,* we tell ourselves. After all, we've never harmed a child, raped a woman, or exposed our private parts on a street corner. We're pretty decent, almost sexually pure, come to think about it.

Such an attitude belittles our own sins, which, no matter how private or seemingly innocuous, still hurt God and others. How do we move, in the early stages of our marriages, from sin in our sexual lives to a fully passionate relationship with our spouses? Four steps will help.

DEAL WITH YOUR BAGGAGE

No person ever enters into a marriage without patterns of sin. Unmet needs often are the fuel for further sin. Sexuality, because of its power both to control and to destroy, is often an area where these patterns will show themselves. Some people are so tied up emotionally, and so damaged, that they are sexually dysfunctional. Professional counseling may be in order. Spouses must become aware of how they each try to control situations, manipulate power, and run from pain. Does the husband try to simply overwhelm the will of his wife? Does the woman pout? What is the reason that the wife does not enjoy sex? Is it because she has been betrayed in the past and is not willing to trust? Why can't the husband enjoy just touching his wife, instead of always having intercourse? Is it because he is numb to, or afraid of, intimacy? Is pleasure all that matters? In order to know and love each other well, we must understand the dynamics of the past and how it has created patterns of sin. If we do not have self-understanding and an understanding of our spouse, we will often be blocked in our attempts to love.

D on't store up grievances. Talk with one another about hurts, problems, and patterns of sin. . . . If you voice your concerns once, and the other spouse doesn't seem to get it, voice them again.

COMMUNICATE, COMMUNICATE, COMMUNICATE

Unless good patterns of communication are set up early in a marriage, a couple is probably headed for disaster. Often, in the emotion and passion of the first few years of marriage, good communication is neglected. The tendency is to either have sex or to fight. Or both. Love—this grand adventure we have set upon together—shouldn't concern itself with the mundane. Love is supposed to conquer all. In such an exalted environment, it seems quite petty to be upset that your husband didn't take the trash out. Or that it takes your wife nearly the time it took Columbus to sail the ocean blue to put on her makeup. After all, why waste your time on such minor complaints when the bed is right upstairs? Everything seems much rosier after an orgasm or two.

Please, listen to me: communicate, communicate, communicate. Deal with your differences immediately. Don't store up grievances. Talk with one another about hurts, problems, and patterns of sin. If you have to schedule a time each week for a "gripe" session, free from the heat of emotions, do it. If you voice your concerns once, and the other spouse doesn't seem to get it, voice them again. Don't ever adopt the attitude "I'll just suppress the things that are bothering me until they go away." They won't. When a person hides a grievance, it will boil and stir, gather other concerns to itself, and come out much the way lava explodes from a volcano.

Not to voice concerns is to be dishonest with your spouse and to erect a marriage-threatening barrier between the two of you. This barrier, fed by other unresolved issues and grievances, will grow over time and make it impossible for you to develop oneness with your spouse. The acid of disappointment and hurt will simply be too great.

SLOW DOWN AND HAVE FUN

Young people are prone to distraction. Causes are great, and energy is high. There is often a temptation early in marriage to let your focus wander: job, ministry, friends. There are so many paths to feeling important, respected, and valued, and the temptation is to take them all. My advice is to keep a check on your motivations: why are you working so hard, or moving so fast? Is it because you are trying to find your value outside of your relationship with Jesus Christ?

Busyness is a fun killer. And once fun disappears from a marriage, anything (or anyone) is likely to follow. It is therefore vital to balance the competing demands in your life, so you can make marriage-building a priority. Do some of the crazy things you did together when you were dating. Remember how good it feels to hold your spouse's hand on a walk around the block. Go out on picnics in the middle of the woods. Find a secluded beach and do . . . well, whatever comes naturally. Life is too short to be driven continually by Day-Timers®, calendars, and watches. Laugh a lot, enjoy each other. True love must rest on trust, honesty, and plain old fun. It is only when those foundations are built and maintained that oneness, the self-giving union of two souls, is possible.

CHAPTER 5

TRANSITION

I like to call them "sex-busters." They can take any number of forms: poor attitudes, overwhelming circumstances, emotional baggage, unresolved conflicts, and/or unattended relationships. But some of the biggest sex-busters often are small. They say "Daddy" and "Mommy" and turn a once peaceful house into a Nightmare on Elm Street. They are known by various names: toddlers, preschoolers, and others that I would just as soon not repeat. Although they are often loving, cute, and can make your day in a second, they can also bring their parents' sex lives to a state of virtual nonexistence.

Nearly by definition, parents of preschool children are out of control. The typical situation often goes as follows. A mother spends her day like a character in a B-grade horror movie: an endless parade of bottles, diapers, dinners, spills, dishes, warnings. The father comes home, exhausted from a day of work, plays with the children, wrestles them into their pajamas, and helps put them to bed. After the tenth glass-of-water-request, the husband and wife drag themselves toward their bedroom. Do you think that either of them has romance on his or her mind? You can bet if one does, the other doesn't. Most likely, the only thing on either of their minds is sleep.

I remember that era in Lynne's and my marriage well. It was like a never-ending nightmare. I remember feeling so disconnected from Lynne I could barely remember what sex was like. I was worried I would forget how to do it. We went through a particularly horrible stretch that lasted about six weeks: earaches, runny noses, various and sundry sicknesses, kids getting up in the middle of the night. It was six weeks of pure madness.

And then one night, out of the blue, it happened. Both kids went to bed and actually fell asleep. It was about 8:00 P.M. I remember the two of us glancing at each other with a look that said, "Now, what do we do?" I got a little gleam in my eye and Lynne got a little gleam in hers, and we walked down the hall toward our bedroom. I remember saying to Lynne, "If we get interrupted tonight, I'm going to kill myself." She said, "Me too." With that, we began. We crawled into bed, and I wrapped my arms around her. What a wonderful feeling. I said, "Oh, so this is what you feel like; this is wonderful." And just as I started to kiss her, *boom*, the bedroom door flew open. Our little girl ran in and vomited all over our bed!

This seems funny now. Back then, it was about as humorous as . . . well, cleaning vomit off the bedspread. But that's the way it often goes with our sex lives. God asks us to be sexual beings in an imperfect world. As the initial hormones and romance fade from our marriages, day-to-day reality steps in, demanding our time, energy, and commitment. No longer is it just "me and you" but "me and you plus the babies, the job, the dog, the church, the bills, and the broken washing machine." Intimacy, once a whisper in the ear, has now given way to the scream of survival.

SUCCESSFULLY WORKING THROUGH PROBLEMS

These are the years that make up the age of transition. Youth is lost; responsibilities are gained. Passion is drained into the day-to-day familiar. Energy is reserved for the urgent, and a spouse is often taken for granted. Roses are what one sometimes sees in a magazine. Romance often seems irrelevant or impractical. This period in a couple's life is critical. Sexuality is likely to grow cold as the coals of intimacy fade. Worse yet, if the coals of romance are not constantly tended, couples can grow apart, and any fire, even a deadly one, may be pursued for just a hint of warmth.

The years just before middle age are a period rife with serious life issues, deteriorating resources, and surfacing problems. The energy of youth and passion are no longer available to prop up denial, hope, and illusion. In no other period in our lives are we so left to ourselves. Couples can no longer delude themselves about the realities of their lives: "My spouse is no longer what she appeared to be, and I am no gem myself." In the presence of such knowledge, we have two options: (1) face the painful facts and, with God's help, move through them to maturity, or (2) seek to escape. One route is painful, but it leads to freedom. The other route seems painless, but it leads to bondage.

Several years into their marriage, Rebecca and her husband continued to struggle sexually. There were still the children to care for. There was still Rebecca's fear of sexuality inbred by her father during her childhood. And there was still her husband's almost incessant sexual hunger. He almost never failed to ruin an intimate dinner by bringing up sex. He was in a state of constant irritation about it, like a man with a popcorn hull stuck in the back of his throat. He'd do sex alone if he could, but he just wasn't designed that way. He needed her body to make it work.

Rebecca was angry that sex was no longer as it was at first, intense and pleasurable. More and more, sex reminded her of her father; she withdrew into her inhibition and fear. Something about sex made her feel dominated, controlled. Dark pictures of sex from her childhood—the anger and paranoia of her father and the stapled pages of her mother's book—kept resurrecting in her mind.

And so they made it a point to fight about it. They knew it was too important to back away from. Says Rebecca, "I'd hate to talk about sex because it just seemed like it took so much work. The conversations we had were about feeling angry, being demanding, and being controlled. These were tough issues to work through because they hit on deep issues in our lives. But, in looking back, those were the very conversations that really counted."

Sex was frustrating because they experienced a degree of intimacy in many areas of their marriage. They truly loved each other. That kept both of them from seeking physical intimacy through affairs. "A lot of times, people look outside their marriage for intimacy and for someone to affirm them," Rebecca says. "We always had that verbal intimacy, even when times were rough and we fought. He complimented me a lot and stayed on my team." For her husband, the pace of life also kept him from adultery. He worked seventy hours a week. When he came home, there were babies to bounce. "I never had the time to think about an affair, let alone have one."

There was no one turning point in their sex lives. There was instead, a gradual change put into motion by a significant shift in two areas of their marriage. For one, they stopped having babies after number four. The act of sex stopped feeling like another mouth to feed. For another, God was at work in their lives. As each of them developed a growing relationship with God, each sought to demonstrate the character of God to the other. Instead of trying to find someone to blame for problems, each sought ways to be responsible. Even though her husband often was frustrated by Rebecca's reluctance when it came to sex, he chose to ask God, "What do you want me to do about this problem?" God showed him his demanding spirit. Just as God was patient, forgiving, loving, and challenging in His dealings with them, so they attempted to be to each other.

It was through the process of individual maturity that they made a discovery that revolutionized their marriage and, eventually, their sex lives. They discovered that marriage is not about me and you, but about us. Just as Christ and the church were one—the Head and the body—so it should be in a marriage. Motivations and actions should revolve around what was best for the new, joint organism. In the light of that discovery selfishness began to look counterproductive. Servanthood became attractive and healthy. "As we tried to serve one another," says Rebecca's husband, "the strength of our marriage increased exponentially."

Slowly, the concept of serving one another began to take hold in their sexuality. It was a long process. They had to deal with the emotional baggage of Rebecca's dysfunctional ideas about sex and her husband's lack of patience for change. Slowly, however, as the rejuvenated sex seeped into their souls, the pages of Rebecca's childhood book on sex, one by one, became unstuck. The design stunned her with its beauty.

Rebecca and her husband took the difficult path. They faced the pain, dissonance, and chaos in their lives and, through a commitment to one another, worked through it. That kind of courage is rare in today's society where you throw away, not fix, things that do not work: a toaster, a contract, a marriage.

Author Scott Peck argues that people will go to unbelievable lengths to avoid pain in their lives. Instead of dealing with problems squarely, people will often ignore them or divert their attention to finding relief through sports, shopping, eating, or drugs. And they are able to create a fairly convincing image of peace and comfort. But the peace is false, and the comfort is costly. It is bought at the expense of reality and personal growth.

In many ways, it makes sense to avoid pain. No healthy human enjoys suffering. Moreover, the issues in our lives that are most likely to create the greatest amount of pain are the ones that are the most stubborn. Anything—compromise, sin, escape, apathy—seems preferable. But that is short-view thinking. If you are going to achieve maturity you are going to have to face painful issues head-on through repentance, obedience, and trust in God. For if you do not deal with problem areas of your life, hurt and anger will entrench themselves in your heart, rooting deeper and later resurfacing to cause even greater damage. As the old television commercial puts it, "You can pay me now, or pay me later."

Often couples feel a twisted sense of security once they become married. The courtship is finished, the "marriage thing" done. Now they can move on to other priorities.

FIVE PROBLEM AREAS

As Lynne and I have traveled, counseled, and talked to other Christians, we have concluded that only about 25 percent of Christian couples have a mutually fulfilling sex life. Although our research is totally unscientific, I believe it is accurate. I believe that most couples simply have not realized God's design for sexuality within their marriages. That fact can be attributed primarily to the failure of people to face painful issues of sin in their lives, issues that most fully emerge and blossom during the years of transition between youth and middle age. I would like to examine just a few of the more serious problem areas.

SELFISHNESS

A good deal of sexual sin, either of omission or commission, is the result of old-fashioned, dyed-in-the-heart selfishness. Selfishness can take many forms. A husband who demands sex (or sexual experimentation) from his wife "as his right" is selfish. A woman who withholds sex from her husband because she is mad about something is selfish. Often such selfishness is symptomatic of a deeper problem, such as a pattern of sin, but often it is not.

I once counseled a couple after the man had committed adultery. I went through my list of standard questions, trying to determine the cause. Do you fight? No. Do you enjoy being with one another? Yes. How are things at work? Fine. Are the children causing any problems? No. How is your sex life? Wonderful. Do you have any bitterness or anger against the other? No. What about the in-laws? We get along great. Do you encourage one another? Yes.

Needless to say, I was getting desperate, so I started asking the questions again, this time pleading with them for the truth. The answers came back the same. But after all the questions had been answered, the husband responded, almost under his breath, "I guess the whole thing was like forbidden fruit." The husband had a problem with emotional and spiritual immaturity; he was selfish. He wanted more than he was entitled to have.

Certain people are more prone to such carnality. Those with low self-esteem will often seek affirmation in an affair, especially if they do not sense an atmosphere of encouragement at home. Those who have been overindulged as children are often prone to affairs. And those with power, money, and control may become enamored with themselves and think they have a right to sexual favors. Many people devote much of their life's energy to achieve the rank where status, respect, and sexual perks are expected.

FAMILIARITY

Familiarity is one of the greatest killers of romance and passion. What once was all roses, phone calls, staying up late, and eating by candlelight becomes a demand to take the trash out. After the first few years of marriage, the spark often disappears into a sea of the mundane: budgets, diapers, morning breath, daily commutes, and meat loaf on Wednesday. Pressures of overly hectic lives continually force the intimacy of marriage onto the altar as the only available sacrifice.

Several factors contribute to the problem of familiarity. The most damaging is our attitudes. Often couples feel a twisted sense of security once they become married. The courtship is finished, the "marriage thing" done. Now they can move on to other priorities. It's not usually a matter of being mean spirited, but practical. There are only so many things that can be done in a day. Why should I now court my spouse, tend to romance, and shower him or her with attention, affirmation, and service? We're already married. So attention is often focused elsewhere, usually on the marketplace or the children.

The damage of such a shift is tremendous. The spouse who once felt treasured now feels taken for granted—the last priority on the list, even if that ranking is unintentional. Self-esteem is demolished. If the hurt is swallowed, anger, resentment, and bitterness take over. If there is any life at all in the couple's sex, it is the equivalent of cooking a pot roast or fixing a leaky roof. Just another chore in another day of an otherwise monotonous marriage.

EMOTIONAL AND PSYCHOLOGICAL BAGGAGE

In the passion and energy of youth, an unusual characteristic of a spouse is often viewed as cute or pleasantly quirky. The uniqueness is attractive. But as the years wear on and middle age approaches, idiosyncrasies become about as attractive as the scratch of fingernails on a chalkboard. Personality issues or patterns of behavior that once might have been overlooked are now recognized as damaging. A husband may place too many expectations on his wife, or a wife may come to dislike sex because she always feels as though she is being used. These surface problems could be symptoms of deeper ones: feeling unloved as a child or being sexually abused.

Many times problem areas in a marriage trace back to a spouse's being raised in a dysfunctional family. Such learned patterns of negative behavior, passed on from generation to generation, are becoming increasingly frequent. Recently I had lunch with a senior statesman of a large missionary organization. He told me that the number one problem he faced was not recruiting enough missionary candidates, but recruiting healthy ones. Thirty years ago, he said, almost all of the candidates came from healthy, stable Christian homes. Now, the situation has changed dramatically. "In almost every case," he said to me, "there has been a divorce, or a case of alcoholism, drug abuse, or sexual abuse. It is the rare exception that we get a couple who is not struggling to cope with a potentially destructive issue of some sort in their marriage."

112

Those issues, although deeply rooted, must be resolved. Otherwise, there will be damage in the home, and the broken baton will be passed to yet another generation.

UNRESOLVED CONFLICTS AND UNMET NEEDS

If you were to come early to our church on Sunday morning, you would hear our band warming up their instruments. The pianist strikes the pitch, and the musicians tune their instruments to that note. If they were to start to play before tuning up, the music you would hear would only be shrill noise, not something pleasant to listen to. People prefer harmony. Dissonance creates tension and anxiety.

When two imperfect people join in marriage, dissonance is a natural result. If these clashes are not dealt with, detachment and disconnection will follow. Slowly but surely, the spouses will pull away from one another. Silence will replace happy chatter, criticism will replace encouragement, and walls will replace bridges. We humans are a needy bunch. We need empathy, love, understanding, and a sense that we are deeply valued. Although it is true that God is the only one who can meet all our needs, it is also true that a spouse, as an image-bearer of God, is capable of meeting the ongoing needs of his or her partner in ways that no other human can.

Unmet needs and unresolved conflicts often feed on one another. If a spouse doesn't feel as though his partner appreciates him, he will often bury the hurt, not realizing the importance of having needs met. The more hurts he swallows, the greater his hunger for satisfaction, the more likely he will reach the point of anger and bitterness. The cycle is deadly and must be broken through honest, precise communication. If it is not, sex will die: it is difficult to undress a person who is wearing a mask, hiding his or her true feelings.

Brad's marriage lasted five years. His wife left him for another man. Brad was not surprised; he realized shortly into the marriage that there would be trouble. When they dated they shared a mutual interest—doing ministry together—but not one another's heart. They had not courted properly. Although each had remained sexually pure during their dating

113

relationship, they had never taken the time to really get to know each other.

Cracks in their relationship appeared quickly. A year into the marriage, Brad lost his job as a Christian counselor. His intense focus on ministry suddenly became only so many idle hours; without activity, he was lost. Eventually, he became introspective, contemplative, self-absorbed. He began to notice faults—both his and those of his wife. He noticed that, beneath the bond of busyness, they had different approaches to life. He was prone to risk taking, independence, and control. His wife was driven by a need to be known by submissive qualities: kind, faithful, sweet, serving. Both wanted the same things—to be respected, valued, and loved—but they chose different methods of achieving those benefits. That was especially true with regard to their relationship to God and to each other.

Both tended to be utilitarian. They needed others because of what they could receive from them. Brad was more aggressive; he had the ability to command the respect and loyalty of others. He was secure enough in his personality and abilities to attract the interest of others. He won by leading.

His wife felt the need to please. Lacking proper self-esteem, she pursued others with an undying attention to serving. No one in the church served more than she did. She won by losing. Both of their motives were disconnected from the love of God, which is selfless, unconditional, and free. They both loved for reasons.

Throughout their marriage, they leaned to extremes. Their sex life tilted between passion and apathy. Brad vacillated between caring and domination, wildness and fear. At his best, he sought to fill his need for intimacy, genuinely experienced as a child, through caring. At his worst, he tried to strip his wife of her inhibitions, demanding that she experiment with new positions and attitudes without providing her with the environment and freedom to change and yet be herself.

Brad often became obsessed with free expression. His wife tried to please Brad. She swallowed her reservations and gave him what she thought he wanted. Although her heart wasn't usually in it, her body was. Brad says she genuinely received pleasure from sex.

"What was missing from our sex was the same thing that was missing in our marriage—intimacy," Brad says. "We were pursuing each other for selfish reasons. I have a tendency to dominate; she has a tendency to submit. It was a deadly combination."

When Brad lost his job, he stopped being busy. Ministry, the tireless effort to help others through his own abilities, was limited. He began to focus more attention on his wife. When he demanded that she slow her life down, she did so, reluctantly; she wanted to please him, especially at such a difficult point in his life. As a consequence, they both became more aware of their own neediness. Brad became more demanding, his wife more passive. Instead of challenging and sharpening one another, they fed into each other's worst tendencies.

From outward appearances, it was not a bad marriage. They seldom had explosive fights. Sometimes they held hands in public. They joined small groups designed to enrich their marriage. "We were trying to figure out how to look good rather than live good," Brad says. "When tension started to come between us, we started to compromise with our expectations for marriage. It was much easier than dealing with the tension and how each of us was contributing to it with our sin."

Brad retreated more frequently into pornography, which he had dabbled with since he was a teenager. It was, he says, far from an obsession, but what had been a two-or-three-times a year escape became a two-or-three times a month habit. "I felt I needed a shot sexually," Brad says. "If I couldn't have intimacy, then I would at least have more pleasure, free and easy. That's what I thought." Often, in order to supercharge sex, he would secretly view pornography before making love to his wife.

Four years into the marriage, Brad got a job in secular counseling, ending two years of on-and-off employment. He pursued his job with all the passion he was capable of. A few months later, his wife met a man who was kind to her. He

*often asked her what she thought. Within six months, they had
an affair. Brad's wife pursued it with all the passion she could.*

For Brad, sex had become a matter of power. At first, he
longed for sex to give him intimacy, that special feeling of love
and connectedness he had experienced as a child in a loving
home. The sex with his wife, as it turned out, wasn't the problem. The problem was that unmet needs, unresolved conflicts,
familiarity, and selfishness blocked their intimacy.

Unwilling to deal with the tension in his marriage, Brad decided to compromise. In sex with his wife he would settle for
pleasure. Although he sought to be tender, sex no longer was a
gift for his wife. It became a tool to meet his needs, a roller
coaster of highs and lows. When Brad and his wife decided to
settle for less than intimacy, they still experienced a great deal
of pleasure. Although neither of them felt closer to the other at
the level of heart and soul, sex often helped to numb the pain.

There is a paradox here. Even when sex fails at the level of
intimacy, it often "succeeds" at meeting other needs. It can, if
nothing else, feed the demands of selfish desires. And couples
who would rather compromise than work through problems often use sex to avoid having to deal with painful issues in their
lives. Each person seeks to meet as many unmet needs as he can
through pleasure and abandonment, which in turn serves to
anesthetize unresolved conflicts. Undiluted passion, stripped
of a giving spirit, becomes the goal and often a major obstacle
to needed change in the relationship.

The same kind of a short-term high is available through pornography. Pinup girls are one-dimensional and offer no hostil-
ity, tension, or commitment—just easy sex, free of commitment. Or so it seems. Pornography is dangerous because it
presents the illusion of safety, of isolated and controlled sin. It
is, as they say, a "victimless" crime as long as it doesn't "hurt"
someone else.

Brad, along with thousands of others, found out differently.
Pornography warps the mind by reducing a person's percep-
tion of and feelings toward women. By its nature, pornography
involves a "user" and a thing "used." One is active, the other
passive. In the mind, there occurs a subtle and powerful shift:

women are no longer complex mysteries of God's creation to be respected, valued, and loved, but degraded slaves to be used —in a sense, "masturbated over."

THE DESIRE TO ESCAPE PRESENT REALITIES

During times of relational tension, sex is powerful for another, nearly opposite, reason. Instead of being used to numb pain, it can be a powerful enticement for a person to leave his or her problems (and spouse) and "come alive" in the arms of another. An affair often offers a twisted promise. The problem, it whispers seductively, is that you married (or at least are having sex with) the wrong person. Why go to all the work of fixing a problem that is probably not fixable? That is a powerful message.

This tendency is especially true in the early stages leading up to an affair, when there is usually a powerful sense of caring, romance, and courting of one another—the very things that are absent in the marriage at this stage. Sex becomes a powerful force fueled by the overwhelming need for intimacy. Intimacy, the lie goes, will happen automatically when I find the right person. The problem really doesn't lie with me or even with my lover, but lies in the fact that up to now neither of us has found the right person.

Sexual temptation, in all of its forms, is incredibly alluring. But please believe me: all that glitters is not gold. At the core of each sexual temptation is a lie straight from hell itself. Don't be fooled; the easy road of escape is the road to bondage. Deal with your sin and problems. Get out before it's too late and the consequences overwhelm your life, your marriage, your self-esteem, your walk with God, your reputation. That will be painful, but it is the journey toward maturity and, consequently, the only road to sexual fulfillment.

Fantasy was at the center of the sex lives of Cathy and John. Reality simply wasn't good enough, or at least no longer in reach. They both treated their spouses as irrelevant to their real sexual hunger. Cathy viewed her husband as kind, but lacking understanding. John saw his wife as fiercely loyal, but slightly overweight and safe. You see, in John's and

117

Cathy's separate situations, no normal lover would do. What was needed was the perfect fantasy lover.

John had such a lover in mind. In his endless road of sexual conquests, he knew exactly what—or who—he was looking for. The girl would look, think, and shine exactly like the first Playboy *centerfold he had ever seen when he was a boy. She would be beautiful, bubbly, and play ball.*

So far, in dozens of sexual encounters, he had not found her. Not even close. Certainly, he had not found her in his wife; she was far too wrapped up with the common, the tasks of the day-to-day. John would know when he met his perfect lover.

In her fantasy life, which was activated more and more by guilt and need, Cathy had several such lovers. They were anchored on real men of power and prestige, people with whom she might have a passing acquaintance and who might have given her a kind word or two—doctors, ministers, choir directors, car dealers. A janitor would never make her list. Power was required, because in Cathy's mind, sex was all about power: the ability to escape, the ability to have unmet needs met, the ability to ensnare others, the ability for self-enhancement.

John found his fantasy lover in a bowling alley. His Playboy *centerfold made flesh. "She had all the qualities," John says, "except she wasn't blonde." John was willing to be flexible. He remembers that he went up to her and asked, "Do you believe in love at first sight?" When she said, "No," he asked: "Do you believe in lust at first sight?" She replied, "Oh, yeah, absolutely."*

John, not particularly religious at this point in his life, was thanking God. Every prayer he had unconsciously uttered found its answer in this woman. Immediately, they fell in lust. It was, beyond his wildest dreams, everything he hoped for and more. She was everything that his wife wasn't: uninhibited, stunningly beautiful, outgoing, a party animal.

John began to scheme to get out of his marriage. He knew what he wanted. Sure, there were a couple of pangs of doubt about the direction of his life. The previous winter, he had been in the hospital. He had a heart condition. "I woke up with all these wires attached to my chest. That gave me some time for introspection." And then there was his life now. At times, he looked almost suicidal: the heavy drinking and smoking had returned since finding his perfect lover. He wondered how he could be so careless.

Also, there were faults in his fantasy woman. He began to notice that she had some annoying traits. But then again, no one was perfect. He was committed, since his early childhood really, to pursuing his fantasy lover.

One weekend he went to a wild party with her in another state. His perfect lover made a perfect fool of herself. John came home, disillusioned, walked his wife up to their bedroom and told her that he had had an affair—just one—and that he wanted their marriage to succeed. At the same time, he wrote his fantasy lover; he wanted that relationship to come to an end.

A month later, he got a call from his lover. She wanted to talk. They met in a restaurant, and one-half hour later they were in bed. A month later, John asked his wife for a divorce. He told her that, after fifteen years of marriage, he did not love her. Never had. He still remembers the look of pain and betrayal on her face: "I couldn't have hurt her more if I had hit her in the stomach with a cement block. That look is permanently etched into my mind." John moved into an apartment. He continued to provide for his wife and two children, but he had nothing to give of himself. He was intent on immersing himself in his guilt, shame, and emptiness.

Cathy, after her conversion to Christianity, remained faithful to her husband. She never slept around again after her affair early in their marriage. She couldn't handle the guilt. Her fantasy life, to a certain degree, protected her. She could fantasize without anyone ever knowing and achieve a certain level of pleasure. It seemed low risk. She even protected herself from her own emotions. "I like to pick people (her fantasy lovers) who are unreachable," she says. "It's almost an addiction to wanting and not having, that sick longing that drives me."

The idea of safe fantasy had turned into a fantasy itself. She had been destroyed by her addiction. The guilt was overwhelming. She entered into Christian therapy to deal with it. Later, she confessed her fantasy lovers to her husband. He wanted reasons; she didn't have any. "I just can't deal with the shame," she says. Her husband chose to stay with the marriage, partly for the children, partly because he cared for his wife. "I feel so much shame," Cathy says, "It's not so much what I have done, but who I am. My whole being is full of shame."

The torment in her soul between her desire for purity in faith and the filthy thoughts of her mind, between her unmet needs and the promises of God, and between the ideas of sex and love has been overwhelming. "My soul is in turmoil," she says.

The sexual sins of John and Cathy represented a retreat from reality into a fantasy world—and temporary relief from unmet needs and conflict. But in the end, the sexual sin, incapable of touching deeper issues, caused still greater damage, creating ever deepening levels of need. That led to more sin, more damage, more need, and more sin.

The cycle they were on is tenacious and vicious. When it is pursued it is almost impossible to break. The soul that seeks escape from pain becomes bonded to a pain beyond anyone's wildest nightmares, if the problem isn't arrested.

THE CONSEQUENCES OF SEXUAL SIN

I can hear some people object: That is the case with sexual addiction, obsession, and perversion. But that's not me. I am just experimenting. I am just trying to be true to myself, to find myself. A little fun, a little escape from my problems may provide me with perspective. Many secular psychologists, in fact, are now encouraging frustrated spouses to engage in "healthy adultery." Dr. Albert Ellis, a prominent sexologist, counsels sexually frustrated couples to commit adultery in order to "rejuvenate" their love lives. This counsel is simply another justification of and rationalization for sin.

The negative consequences of sexual sin are almost too numerous to list. I know of one man, however, who, when facing sexual temptation, attempts to do just that. He reviews in his mind the cost of sexual sin:

- Dragging Christ's reputation into the mud.
- Having to one day look Jesus in the face at the judgment seat and tell why I did it.
- Untold hurt to Nanci, my best friend and loyal wife.
- Loss of Nanci's respect and trust.
- The possibility that I could lose my wife and my children forever.
- Hurt to and loss of credibility with my beloved daughters, Karina and Angie. ("Why listen to a man who betrayed Mom and us?")
- Shame to my family. ("Why isn't Daddy a pastor anymore?" The cruel comments of others who would invariably find out.)
- Shame and hurt to my church and friends, and especially those I've led to Christ and discipled. (List names.)
- An irretrievable loss of years of witnessing to my father.
- Bringing great pleasure to Satan, God's enemy.
- Possibly contracting a sexually transmitted disease (gonorrhea, syphilis, herpes, or AIDS), passing on the disease to Nanci, pregnancy (with its personal and financial implications, including a lifelong reminder of sin to me and my family).
- Loss of self-respect, discrediting my own name, and invoking shame and lifelong embarrassment upon myself.[1]

Seen in this light adultery hardly sounds "healthy." I could not begin to tell you how often I have heard a person say, "I wish I could turn back the clock." Not long ago a businessman sat in my office and wept openly. Thirteen years ago, on a business trip, he had committed adultery with a woman he met in a lounge. For all those years, he carried around with him the burden, the guilt, and the horror of his betrayal. He told me what it had done to his marriage and his spiritual life. He could hardly pray anymore.

FACING THE TRUTH AND REPENTING

Sexual sin can paralyze a person with guilt and shame. If the sin is not repented of, the person must devise some other way to deal with the sin. The path not cut by repentance is the road to spiritual deterioration. I have seen it replayed again and again. After the sexual sin, guilt sets in. Overwhelming guilt. In order to deal with the guilt, the person develops a

121

hard heart. He or she then becomes apathetic, and apathy, allowed to run its careless course, results in self-deception. Soon the person is no longer able to discern truth from lie, reality from fantasy. "That's your definition of adultery," one is likely to say. Or, "If my spouse had met my needs, I wouldn't have had to have an affair." Self-deception, if not dealt with, will lead to spiritual desertion from God.

> Repentance involves feeling the gravity of sins and accepting the consequences. It also involves changing behavior. The sin is so grievous to the person that he or she will do everything in his or her power to keep it from happening again.

King David chose the road of repentance after committing adultery with Bathsheba and killing her husband. Listen to the words of David as recorded in Psalm 38:4–8, 17–18 (NASB):

> For my iniquities are gone over my head; as a heavy burden they weigh too much for me. . . . I am bent over and greatly bowed down; I go in mourning all day long. For my loins are filled with burning; and there is no soundness in my flesh. I am benumbed and badly crushed; I groan because of the agitation of my heart. . . . My strength fails me; and the light of my eyes . . . has gone from me. My loved ones and my friends stand aloof from my plague; and my kinsmen stand afar off. . . . For I am ready to fall, and my sorrow is continually before me. . . . I am full of anxiety because of my sin.

Repentance, real repentance, is not a matter of muttering a few words under your breath—"Oh, I'm sorry"—and going on with life. Repentance involves feeling the gravity of sins and accepting the consequences. It also involves changing behavior. The sin is so grievous to the person that he or she will do everything in his or her power to keep it from happening again. God's grace for David, His restoring power, came only after David felt the full weight of his sin.

Sometimes we paint too rosy a picture of God; we embroider verses about God's love, mercy, and tenderness and frame them in wall plaques. All of that is true, but it begs for balance. Hebrews 10:31 (NASB) states, "It is a terrifying thing to fall into the hands of the living God." The verse refers to falling into God's hand of judgment after disobedience. It is terrifying to fall into the hands of the living God, because we fall utterly short of His complete holiness. He has the right and the means to exact terrible retribution from us for our sins. Our sins defy His holiness on a vast scale.

Few people take God's wrath seriously, but God's anger is real. The pattern in the Bible is that when people committed adultery, God chastised them. King David lost the infant child born to Bathsheba as a result of his adultery with her. I'm not saying God always disciplines that severely, but I am saying He has a right to do anything. God will not be mocked.

Moreover, He loves us too much to allow us to continue in our folly. Hebrews 12:10 says, "[God] disciplines us for our good, that we may share His holiness" (NASB). Sin leads to self-destruction, but holiness leads to abundant life. God knows this and is willing to employ a firm hand of discipline in order to protect us from continued sinful choices.

These sinful choices, when perpetuated, lead not only to self-destruction but, even more tragically, to the destruction of others. Stories such as Janine's remind us that unleashed sin always leaves a suffering victim.

When Janine was admitted to the hospital after the flashbacks of sexual abuse began, she figured she would be there a week. Maybe two, tops. Then, she could get on with her life. Seven weeks later she was still in the hospital and still wanted to kill herself. She knew then that she was in it for the long haul.

"Physically," Janine says, "I am healed. I have no scars, no remnants of the abuse. Everything works. The horrendous part of sexual abuse is not what it does to a person's body, but what it does to a person's mind, emotions, and soul."

Sexual aggression is incalculably destructive and distorts the child's thinking about sex at the very time he or she is trying to learn the vocabulary of relationship. A father who says he loves his child and then has sex with her has twisted forever the verb "love" in her mind. Instead of trust, safety, and tenderness, the concepts that are ingrained in her thinking about sex become betrayal, control, and devastation.

At first, Janine merely fought to survive. The terror overwhelmed her. She had dissociated so completely from the events that when they finally emerged in her consciousness when she was thirty they came "out of the blue." Until that point she had no clue that sexual abuse had been part of her life.

In an effort to survive, her mind had made clean work of the abuse, hiding it beneath the level of conscious awareness. But as she grew older, she lost all connection with joy. "I was a flatliner," Janine says of her life before the flashbacks came. "I lived life like the flat line on one of those heart machines—no ups or downs. I was really dead."

The desire for something more, she believes, began to trigger the flashbacks. In order for her to experience life, the vibrant life that goes beyond self-protection, she had no choice but to move through the pain.

Her first hospital stay lasted two and a half months. She couldn't sleep, unless medicated. She couldn't eat, unless forced. As each new memory appeared, she questioned her sanity. That couldn't have really been her in the flashbacks. She had to be crazy to think so.

She was out of the hospital for a few weeks, then back in. She remembers sitting on the gray floor of the hospital room, breaking down in tears. She was emotionally and spiritually paralyzed: "I can't do anything," she cried. "I am of value to no one." She pleaded with her husband to divorce her. To get a wife who wasn't such a mess.

She felt an overwhelming sense of loneliness: "No one could face those flashbacks for me. I was in the battle alone. The loneliness, the feeling of being abandoned, was absolutely terrifying." She lost touch with God. In her mind, He had become the enemy. First, He had allowed the abuse. Second, He was a father Himself. And like her father, He had incredible power. Power to abuse. Or power to stop the abuse. Both God and her father claimed to love her but acted as though they didn't care. Janine allowed herself the freedom to be honest with herself and with God.

Suicide was a way to end the pain. "I always made sure I left myself that option," she says. "It was a form of control for me." But once the terror changed into rage Janine began the fight in earnest. She resolved to regain the child within herself, to free little Janine from her prison of abuse.

The fight has been difficult. In her nearly seven-year struggle to recover, she has experienced agoraphobia, claustrophobia, fear of women, further dissociations, self-abuse, obsessive-compulsive disorders, character changes, acting out, panic attacks, depression. Name a neurosis and, odds are, she has experienced it. She has experienced anger, rage, shame, guilt, terror, alienation, anxiety, and hatred. She has been unable, at times, to forgive, trust, love, and heal. For three years, she could not have sex with her husband; she could not trust, despite his best efforts to love her. She has been disconnected, in very real ways, from those she cared for the most. She has experienced the depths of pain.

And, occasionally, a peculiar joy. She made a friend, her first real one. She opened up herself to this person out of desperation and pain, risking the depths of her soul. One time, they went to the shopping mall together. They took along a blank cassette tape and crammed themselves into one of those Record-A-Song booths. Neither one of them could sing worth a hoot. Janine giggled herself silly. She recognized it as the giggle of a little girl.

That spontaneous, childlike giggle is a beautiful reminder that healing can occur, even in a life nearly destroyed by the ugliest, most perverse form of sexual sin. But the journey toward such healing leads one through a mine field of terrifying memories; the work it requires is exhausting. Why, during the years when Janine should be free to love and enjoy her husband and children, is she forced into a daily struggle for survival? Because the gift of sex was twisted in the hands of evil men and women and used as a tool of overpowering violence. Every divine intention regarding human sexuality was turned upside down and devoted to the destructive purposes of the Evil One.

Yes, Janine's story is extreme. But it shares with innumerable other stories these basic truths: Sexual sin produces pain. Sexual sin diminishes life. Sexual sin violently overturns the purposes of God.

NOTE

1. Randy C. Alcorn, *Sexual Temptation: How Christian Workers Can Win the Battle* (Downers Grove, Ill.: InterVarsity, 1989), 29–30.

CHAPTER 6

MATURITY

I f we are to mature in our sexuality, the starting place must be the value God places on human life. The biblical imagery of sex—the union of Christ and the church and its parallel in the union of a man and a woman—shows how closely we are related to God. We are to be united with Christ as His bride, as well as to another human, as a bearer of God's image. When we understand the value of each person, and the profound imagery of sexual union, we will begin to understand the enormity of the gift of sexuality and the responsibilities connected with it.

BRAD

In his mind, Brad views sex with suspicion. His old girlfriend, in part, had killed herself because of it. His ex-wife, in part, had left him because of it. "I know that sex is not the real issue; I know that it goes much deeper than that," Brad says. "But I find it difficult to understand God's design for sex."

For Brad, the only thing more troubling than sex is no sex. Approaching forty, he has been abstinent for three years. "On my bad days," he says, "I really have a hard time believing that God commands single people to go without sex. It seems like a really, really bad idea." But Brad is seeking to be obedient.

A great deal has changed since his marriage failed and his wife left him for another man. First of all, he has been broken in the depths of his being. There was, of course, the sin of his wife. Adultery, regardless of motivation, creates pain like nothing else: "Even though our marriage was not the best," Brad says, "when I found out she had committed adultery, I was devastated. I think she could have much less painfully cut open my chest and pulled out my heart."

Then, there was, and is, his sin. He has come to understand a pattern of behavior that seeks to order life according to his own terms, his own agenda. He seeks and demands control. Part of the reason, he knows, stems from the way he was raised: much of his life has been an overreaction to his father's reluctance to let him make decisions on his own as a child.

But Brad knows that is not an excuse. Sin is still sin. Through repentance, he has learned that it is better to live an abundant life in Christ than a self-seeking life based solely on his own desires. He is seeking to understand and change his need for control. More and more, he wants to yield to God's leadings.

While he seeks to become self-aware, he is trying to avoid becoming self-absorbed. He knows the key to joy is through giving of himself. His needs, he has painfully learned, will never be met outside of an abandonment to the will of God. As God enters into his life, Brad feels loved, valued, and respected. "The more you understand about God's love for you," Brad says, "the more you are able to love others."

In his lay ministry at the church (he is still employed as a secular counselor), Brad is finding deep purpose. "I think I have less motivation now to serve others out of selfish and subtle motivations," Brad says. "Because my relationship with God is growing, I feel less need for other things in my life. That frees up my motivation for ministry. More and more, I can serve and love simply because I want to love."

When it comes to his sexuality, Brad often feels overwhelmed. "There is so much pressure in our society to have sex for the sake of having pleasure," Brad says. "It's very difficult to resist when everyone around you says indulge." The transition for Brad from married to single was traumatic. "Once you are used to sex, even if it isn't particularly intimate, it is difficult to go back to abstinence."

Brad often used pornography to fill the sexual void created by the passage from married to single: at least the fantasy of the activity itself, he believed, quieted the violence of the transition. "I bought the lie that pornography is a victimless sin," he says. "But I was the victim. My view of women became distorted. It was based less on value and respect and more on superficial issues. The only thing that was important was feeding my lust." He has attempted to eliminate pornography from his life, although he still occasionally falls to the sin. "God is at work," he says. "I know that I will eventually gain victory."

Brad is attempting to channel his sexual energy into other areas of his life. Sex, after all, is not just an act you do when you are naked and in bed. The full meaning of sex has little to do with a physical act, but rather involves the building of love, trust, commitment, faithfulness, and caring. Since his abstinence has started, he has found himself establishing many deeper relationships in his life.

But that's not to say he has fallen in love with abstinence. Most of the time he hates it. On soft summer nights, when the moon is half full and three quarters high, he often thinks of his former wife. The way they touched on the beach. The way they folded into each other's arms, sleeping until late into the morning. The way they shared love. "Even though we didn't know how to love each other very well," he says, "we had some tender, sexual moments. Even through our sin, the love was able to shine through." Brad misses those moments.

The deeper meaning and broader value of sexuality must be clearly understood by those who, like Brad, cannot have sex, either because they are not married or because of an illness or incapacity on the part of their spouse. The apostle Paul suggested that for some people it might be better to remain single. In 1 Corinthians 7:32–34, he writes: "I would like you to be free from concern. An unmarried man is concerned about the Lord's affairs—how he can please the Lord. But a married man is concerned about the affairs of the world—how he can please his wife—and his interests are divided." Paul is saying that the ideal union, the best state of being, is oneness with Christ: complete and undistracted devotion.

The energy, passion, longing, commitment, and devotion that is inherent in our sexuality, expressed through intercourse, can be given to God; in so doing, the gift of sexuality He gave us is offered back to Him as act of service and worship. I have seen single people, although only a few, who have successfully channeled their sexual energy into their relationship with God. Because they are undistracted in focus, they are wholeheartedly devoted to God. Such singles are satisfied with their singleness and enjoy a special focus on Christ. They are at peace with themselves, mature and fulfilled.

But that kind of single is rare. Many singles just cannot handle their sexual energy constructively. It is as though they have sexual time bombs strapped to their bodies, wired to explode at any moment. Most of these singles are single by circumstance. Like Brad, many are divorced and accustomed to having sex. But it is not just the sex that drives them; they long for intimacy and an end to their loneliness. They hate being alone on Christmas. They dream of being able to come home to a warm hug and a bed to share. They understand all of God's restrictions, and on good days believe those restrictions are for their own good. On bad days, the hunger to reach out and touch others overpowers them.

Please, understand me: I am not trying to downplay the feelings of disappointment, sexual frustration, and loneliness that most singles experience. As I suggest alternatives to sexual involvement, I do so with full recognition of the difficulty of the discipline God has set before you. But, at the same time, I also

130

understand enough of the Bible to know that those whom God challenges the most are also those to whom He gives opportunities for great service and devotion to Him. Maturity depends on how much we yield to His leading.

FOCUS ON KINGDOM BUILDING

My first suggestion has already been mentioned: seek to channel your sexual energy into kingdom building. Jesus Christ summed up all of God's laws into two: (1) love God with all your heart, mind, soul, and strength; and (2) love others as yourself. To repeat what has been said elsewhere in this book: love involves the giving of oneself to another. Whether this is done through sexuality or through service, it is still an expression of love. The energy of your sexuality can be channeled into self-giving and into healthy and loving relationships with God and others, without sexual expression.

A starting point is to take advantage of fellowship opportunities in your church and attend worship services regularly.

BE OBEDIENT

My second suggestion is to devote yourself wholeheartedly to obedience. No matter how much you give yourself to God and others and mature in the faith, there will still be days when sexuality will almost overpower you. Your whole body, mind, and soul will scream for intimacy, companionship, and sex. During these times of severe temptation, flat-out obedience is the only responsible path you can take. Recall the faithfulness of God. Understand how much He values, loves, and respects you. And remind yourselves of the consequences of sexual sin. As you genuinely desire to overcome sexual temptation, God will give you power along the way.

DO NOT RUSH INTO MARRIAGE

My third suggestion is to not rush into marriage. So often I see singles get married primarily because of a driving need for intimacy and sex. I have counseled enough shattered people to know that a marriage motivated primarily by such needs almost always ends in disaster. If you don't believe anything else that I say, believe this: your feelings of misery as a single are nothing compared to the misery of being in a bad marriage.

SEE YOURSELF AS GOD SEES YOU

My final suggestion is to understand and see yourself as God sees you. He longs to be in deep relationship with you and meet your every need. He treasures you like no one else. He is incapable of damaging those He loves. All His actions and thoughts toward you are designed to make you all He created you to be.

JANINE

Even after seven years of intensive therapy, Janine prays an almost unconscious prayer during sex: Please, God, don't let me flashback. Keep the abusers away. *When she has sex with her husband, she always leaves the lights on. She plays music. She is always in need of orientation, of knowing that she is an adult choosing to have sex and not a terrified little girl being forced to. Most of the time, it works; on occasion she has actually been able to enjoy sex. But that's about it.*

Through the sin of evil people, Janine's vocabulary has been distorted and limited. Don't bother talking to her about the biblical idea of "oneness." It might as well be a foreign word. "Oneness to me," she says, "is being one with an animal, because that's what my abusers tried to do to me." And then there's the word love. *That's what her father used to tell her—and then raped her.*

As hard as she tries to rewire her thinking, she often comes back to the words as she learned them as a child. The sexual violations she experienced as a child completely defined her relational vocabulary: love *means using,* sex *means power over another, and* trust *means betrayal. Janine knows, more than most, of the power of sexuality to distort, warp, and destroy.*

She has been in intensive therapy: two to three times a week for more than seven years. As she has dealt with the bits and pieces of flashbacks she has experienced, she has had to face the full horror of her childhood and attempt, as best she can, to move through the pain. She is trying, with all the strength she can muster, to rescue the little girl inside her. If the little child's hope dies, her childlike ways will also perish—her spontaneity, her joy, her trust in God and life.

She had to first believe that the little girl was worth saving. No one else did, she thought; not even God. "God could have saved me from the abuse," she says, "but He didn't." To this day Janine faces an overwhelming battle to maintain self-esteem.

Her relationship with God is far from where she wants it to be. She still remains angry. "I talk to God now and then. I am absolutely angry at God. I don't understand how He could have allowed this to happen. I hope and believe that those pictures I have of Him deep down inside of me are not true—that they can't be true. Despite my doubts, I have still been able to retain a small, soft part in my heart for Him." Her faith, she says, is "more real and less intellectual."

Despite the pain and doubt, there has been progress. The pain she has experienced has taught her about joy. "I don't think a person can understand the heights of joy until she has experienced the depths of pain." Her life is less "perfect" now than it was before the flashbacks began. She doesn't always say the right thing, act the right way, or care that much about what others think. She is less concerned about living up to other people's expectations and more focused on being real. She has fewer relationships than before, but nearly all of them are at the level of heart-to-heart.

She wishes the healing wouldn't take so long. "I wish I could understand God and love Him. All around me I see people trusting Him and praising Him, and I wish I could do it as well as they do. I really do."

There is cause for hope, although as yet she has been unable to rescue the little girl who was Janine. Through the sexual abuse, Janine pictures that little girl as being put into a bare room in her mind with no lights, windows, furniture, or doors. She is stuck, terrified, and alone. Through the process of healing, she says, she has been able to install a window or two, some toys, and a door. Every once in a while, the little girl has been allowed to walk into other rooms in Janine's mind and explore. She has come out to play. And that little girl, who is a part of her, has changed the way Janine lives life.

Janine knows that the process of change will continue. "I have more battles ahead as I fight to regain the child within me—not the one who was turned into a rag doll, but the one who was born to be fun and loved and loving and respected and strong and fully alive. With Christ's patience, I will be transformed from a victim to a survivor. And I will be free."

ACKNOWLEDGE THE DAMAGE

Janine's biggest struggle is to regain a recognition of her value in the eyes of God. When she was first learning about relationships as a child, the satanic message was conveyed to her: you are a slut, you are no good, you are less than an animal. Part of the road to recovery from abuse of this kind is to squarely face what has occurred and to recognize the huge chasm between the forgiveness of sin and the consequences of sin. God can forgive us, and we can forgive others, but forgiveness does not wipe out the short-term or long-term consequences of sexual sin, be they physical, emotional, or spiritual. We must acknowledge and work through those consequences. Not to do so is to strip the hope of joy from the heart and to live life as what Janine called a "flatliner," someone unable to experience much of anything, living in days of gray.

Not acknowledging the damage of sin will have another effect. Sin will disconnect the person from others in anger, frustration, judgment, and withdrawal. Sex, which is meant to be an expression and celebration of oneness, will be limited by the width of the chasm that it is asked to cross.

Consider, also, Mary. After twenty-five years of marriage and three children, her husband decided to have an affair. When pressed for a reason, he said he needed some fun in his life. Things were too predictable. Regardless of motivation, adultery is a grievous and damaging crime, so much so that the Bible offers an escape clause for those whose spouses commit adultery. They are free to leave the marriage. I believe this is so because God is aware of the severe amount of damage left in adultery's wake. A marriage shaken by this affront will have a difficult time moving forward because adultery undermines the very foundations of a marriage: trust, covenantal loyalty, and mutual respect.

Such a marriage can, however, be repaired. But not through "easy" forgiveness. Mary cannot merely say that she, through the grace of God, forgives her husband. That would be fundamentally unrealistic on her part, denying the reality of sin's destructiveness. Before she can move forward in forgiveness, she must understand how she has been damaged.

She must realize, for example, that her ability to trust has been nearly paralyzed. If she doesn't become aware of the damage, she will not understand her reactions, which often follow the path of self-protective sin. For example, because Mary's trust has been broken in her marriage, she may find herself withdrawing from any relationship or situation that demands the vulnerability of self-giving. Recognition of the effects of sins against us is often a prerequisite for recognizing our own sinful response to that sin.

TURN THE DAMAGE OVER TO GOD

But recognition is not enough. The damage must be turned over to God. Damage has been done, and healing is necessary. If Mary can understand and feel the power of sin, she will be more likely to experience the power of God's grace. Real healing, achieved through the process of honest grief, requires more than the application of a smooth emotional salve; it comes through nothing less than the blood of Jesus Christ.

SEEK GOD'S HELP TO RECAPTURE AN AWARENESS OF HIS LOVE

As Mary seeks healing for her wounds, she must also pray to recapture a sense of God's love. Even though sin has sought to spoil the treasure, God still loves her with the same surprising and inexplicable intensity. Nothing she can do (or that can be done to her) will separate her from the love of Christ. Each person is of incalculable value in the eyes of God. Once Mary begins to stand firm again in the love of God, she will be better equipped to pursue reconciliation.

CLEARLY VOICE YOUR HURT AND CONFESS
YOUR OWN SINFUL RESPONSES TO THAT HURT

Mary must also pursue an ongoing and deep level of communication with her husband. She must clearly voice her hurt as well as confess her own sinful responses to the damage that has been done to her. Her husband must seek to determine and understand the real motivation for his adultery, communicate those reasons clearly to his wife, and seek forgiveness.

BE PATIENT

Finally, there must be patience. Damage from the sin of adultery, both active and reactive, does not disappear overnight. Only the grace of God, *over time,* will fully repair the harm done. Each spouse must determine in his mind to be devoted first to God, tapping into His power for healing and forgiveness, and then to his spouse. Without a full-scale commitment to patience and to loving one another in spite of the damage, the wounds to the marriage will not heal.

CATHY AND JOHN

Cathy and John have each spent a lifetime looking for their childhood homes. A place as it should have been: safe, secure, loving, touching. As a child, Cathy remembers crawling up on the dryer and looking out the window for Daddy to come home from the bars. "I would count the cars, and count the cars, but he would never come home." She says she is still looking out the window. John, trapped by his allergies and his father's distance and death, has looked for someone to love him as a father should, unconditionally. "What I was looking for in all the affairs was for someone to love me for who I was. I had the inner mind-set that I was not worthy to be loved."

The search for such love was acted upon early in their sexuality. Sexuality was close to intimacy, even closer to escape. They used it often, early, and with many benefits. They were able to move people with sex—if not to love, then to strong and sometimes negative emotions. They started to crave the craving. They began to confuse sex with what they really wanted, love. Soon, fantasy, out of necessity, controlled their lives. More and more was needed for less and less.

John had his fling with his fantasy lover, his Playmate made flesh. Yet it filled him with disappointment: fantasy loses its luster in the transition to reality. She was selfish, driven, alcoholic, neurotic—you name it. Self-indulgence, he learned in more ways than one, leads to self-destruction.

Early in their short-lived affair, his fantasy lover asked John to go to church with her. Even though she had almost no sense of morals or commitment to any kind of truth, she always went to church. Churchgoing made her feel cleaner, almost good. John hated her church, a liturgical maze of kneeling and standing; she suggested that he find a better one. He had heard of a church not far away called Willow Creek, a corporate-looking building in the suburbs of Chicago. They decided to go together.

She hated it; he was stunned. "I remember that first message like it was yesterday," John says. "The pastor said something that has stuck with me ever since: 'You matter to God, no matter what.'" God loved him, even if he hated himself. That was the message he had wanted to hear all his life.

Cathy has heard that same message for more than twenty years: that she matters to God. And she has heard of God's promises to fill the void in her soul. But she says she has yet to feel anything permanent. She has been unable to totally free herself from her addiction. Although she has remained faithful to her husband through twenty-three years of marriage, she has retreated once again into her fantasy world of perfect and powerful lovers. She has felt, and still feels, tremendous amounts of interconnected emotion: anger, guilt, shame, resentment, fear, feelings of power, pain, and isolation.

"I'm tied up in knots," she says. More than anything, she says, she wants to follow God. But she has been driven, again and again, by a need that moves her far away from reality. This is a poem she composed about the war zone that is her soul:

My Soul, tired and beaten
By the torrential downpour of reality,
Seeks shelter
In the warm, pulsating compulsion of fantasy
Where needs are met, desire fulfilled
And satisfaction felt.
Where the hole inside grows deeper and deeper
As I vainly struggle to fill it.

As was also true for Cathy, the world that John knew was starting to come apart. Part of the damage was already done: the look in the eyes of his children when he told them he and their mother were getting a divorce; his son was thirteen at the time, the same age John was when his father died. Part of it was that his lifestyle, founded on lies and self-deception, was starting to "clang and not ring true." Part of it was the indecent exposure of his "perfect" lover at a party they had attended together out of state. Mostly, it was this: through John's brokenness, God was getting into his life.

Both Cathy and John have fought fierce battles with their addictions. Much of this battle has been in the form of intensive professional counseling and therapy, for John as often as three times a week. Both confessed sexual sins to their spouses. Both received forgiveness. Both faced the pain of the consequences of their sin. Says John, "I lived my whole life based on a lie. That is a difficult admission to make."

Both want to be clean. They fight against the sexual addiction that has had both of them in its lock since childhood. "What I would like is for someone to understand how difficult, how excruciating this process is," Cathy says.

After years of struggle, John is close to being free of his addiction. He is united in heart, mind, body, and soul with his wife, whom he once almost divorced. He eventually has found in her a human incarnation of what he wanted most: unconditional love. He has stopped the affairs, the pornography, the masturbation, the endless cycle of destruction. He is committed to staying free. He won't even go in front of a mirror without clothes on. That's how careful he is.

He is still dealing with the consequences of a life of sin. The damage he has done is multidimensional: he has caused his wife and kids pain, he has hurt the heart of God, he has difficulty in feeling forgiven, and he has lost an essential part of who he is. "Through unrestrained sex, I have left little bits of myself all over the place, and I can never get all of myself back." Never, this side of heaven.

Cathy also knows of the damage of sexual addiction. She feels the pain in her heart every day. Still, she says, the war rages. After twenty months free from masturbation and sexual fantasy, she recently met a man. He was in one of her support groups. He is an alcoholic, working man, with a tragic childhood—a duplicate of her father. She says he "is thrilling my whole being with his wonderful, necessary words."

She now fantasizes about him, almost continually. She feels trapped, separated from God, and drawn by her lust. "I know that what I am doing is self-destructive," she says. "But I don't want to even look at the consequences."

John is now free to make love. That's the best thing, he says. "I have the joy of making love to my wife. I have the joy of intimacy, of soul-to-soul connection." They will soon celebrate their twenty-fifth wedding anniversary.

Entrapped in sin and addiction, Cathy says that after twenty-three years, she is almost certain she will have an affair. One more vain attempt to make fantasy reality. "It won't work," she says. "I know better."

Christianity and our culture agree that we are damaged people, but are in disagreement as to the cause and the cure. The Bible states that sin is responsible for the damage we see about us. The world uses a different vocabulary for the cause: circumstances, bad genes, accidents. The Bible says sin must be faced and repented of; our culture says we should dismiss personal responsibility for sin and see ourselves simply as victims.

Our culture attempts to repair the human damage but strips it from the context of sin, both personal and collective. Because we have been so damaged, our culture says, we surely cannot be held responsible. There is here an underlying and morbid tone of fate and hopelessness.

This victim mentality is responsible for the high number of addicted people in our society. Because they have been damaged by the sin of others, they seek relief in escape. To avoid the pain and hurt of another's sin, they divert their energies to self-protective or self-destructive strategies, which seek safety or adventure. Such seemingly opposite strategies share the common thread of self-absorption. In either case, the risky and self-abandoning alternatives of love, hope, and faith are often seen as too dangerous and impractical.

Such has been the case with John and Cathy. Early on, sin created damage in their lives, giving birth to overwhelming need. In an effort to meet the need and at the same time avoid further pain, they sought relief through escape. Basing their lives on fantasy—trying to meet their needs through that which was not real—led, of course, to addiction, paralysis, and turmoil of soul. Because they were so focused on their own needs, their sin created enormous damage in the lives of others.

Once a person has given over to an addiction—has made himself a victim of it—he becomes less than fully human. Sin has run its course: the distortion of God-given desire, the reduction of others as objects to meet selfish demands, and the waste of human potential.

REBECCA

God sent His son to die for us and to be resurrected with great power. The same power that resurrected Jesus from the dead is now available to help each one of us die to sin and live in Jesus Christ. It is only then, as we yield our wills to His, that the downward cycle of sin can be broken and love can begin its healing work.

Once Rebecca and her husband began to move toward oneness, the temptations changed. No longer did selfishness appear blatantly. Instead, it came disguised in good intentions, always with a heart for another. Rebecca's husband, passionately in love with her, risked putting her on the throne of his heart. God got squeezed out at times. They both be-

came evangelists, but the banner read "Oneness" and not always "Jesus Christ."

They had zeal, but not a lot of knowledge. "We knew what was happening in our marriage," Rebecca says, "and we wanted others to experience that." They began a small group in their church and started teaching about oneness and intimacy in marriage. As it turned out, they learned that they had a good deal more to learn. Mainly about Jesus Christ.

Psychology, Christian books, marriage enrichment classes: all of these were helpful. But they paled in importance to a growing and transforming relationship with Jesus Christ. "It is only as we are cleansed individually of our selfishness and sin that we are able to better reflect love to one another," says Rebecca's husband. Ezekiel 36:25–26 has become the centerpiece of their marriage: "I will sprinkle clean water on you, and you will be clean; I will cleanse you from all your impurities and from all your idols. I will give you a new heart and put a new spirit in you; I will remove from you your heart of stone and give you a heart of flesh."

And the condition of the heart depends upon Jesus Christ. "Good sex," says Rebecca, "is all about two hearts that are in love with Jesus Christ. When a heart is filled with love for Jesus Christ, it looks for ways to serve others and express love." Sex, they say, is one of God's most powerful, creative and unique gifts. Through it, one person can demonstrate, powerfully and exclusively, love for another.

For Rebecca, good sex is not always possible. With four children still at home, sometimes it's just a matter of timing. Other times, her inhibitions and fears, instilled in her childhood, haunt her; at those times, sex still has the aftertaste of the forbidden. But often, in occasional peaks of grace, she experiences sex as it was meant to be: the celebration of oneness with another, in heart, mind, soul, and body. Rebecca and her husband are learning what it means to take their fig leaves off, stand naked and vulnerable before one another, and, in the light of God's grace, feel unashamed. It is only then that their definition of intimacy—to know and be known—enters the realm of reality.

Sometimes, it takes the form of an orgasm. Sometimes, a smile.

The biblical definition of love is given in 1 Corinthians 13:

> Love is patient, love is kind. It does not envy, it does not boast, it is not proud. It is not rude, it is not self-seeking, it is not easily angered, it keeps no record of wrongs. Love does not delight in evil, but rejoices with the truth. It always protects, always trusts, always hopes, always perseveres.

This love is the antonym of sin. Where love is patient, kind, and humble, sin is impatient, unkind, and proud. Where love is not rude, self-seeking, or easily angered, sin is all of those. Where love does not delight in evil and rejoices in the truth, sin springs from evil and hides from the truth. Where love always protects, trusts, hopes, and perseveres, sin sometimes does too—"as long as there is something in it for me."

Where sin tears down, love builds up. Rebecca and her husband learned to treasure one another and incorporate love's qualities in their lives. They began to see love as a valuing and empowering of one another. Slowly, they learned to put into practice the difficult words of Philippians 2:3–4: "Do nothing out of selfish ambition or vain conceit, but in humility consider others better than yourselves. Each of you should look not only to your own interests, but also to the interests of others."

That is painful work, especially in marriage: internal frictions annoy us; external pressures distract us; poor communication confuses us. We are tempted, with each passing hour, to compromise and settle for isolation and self-interest. We want to settle for less than love in its purest, most giving form.

PRACTICAL STEPS

Many of you may have already given up, or at least determined long ago to settle for less. Your sex life, when there is any at all, is a matter of going through the same motions. You believe there is simply no way back to passion. I am here to tell you there is.

I am not promising it will be easy; in fact, the process will involve single-minded obedience to the will of God. But there are steps you can take to put the oneness back into marriage, and the sizzle back into the bedroom.

> Lynne and I have recognized that we will have inevitable periods of disconnection in our lives. We have determined not to panic during such times, [but call them] "commitment" phases [because we] understand that we are committed to one another for the long haul and will do whatever is necessary to become connected again.

COMMUNICATE

First of all, learn to communicate. This is important when you are newly married, and that is why I mentioned it in the chapter on passion earlier in this book, but it bears emphasis here, too. Many times spouses drift away from one another simply because they don't know one another anymore. They don't know each other's thoughts, dreams, faith, and day-to-day lives. I believe it is critical for couples, regardless of how long they have been married, to have at least one date night each week, with time set aside just for talking—about goals, disappointments, hopes, grievances—yesterday, today, and to-morrow. Romance starts with knowledge of one another, and knowledge comes through communication.

COURT ONE ANOTHER

Couples should also rediscover how to court one another creatively and how to have fun together. With the pressures of raising children, holding down a job, and staying one step ahead of life, the fun often disappears. Marriage, instead of a refuge, often becomes part of the routine, another cause of exhaustion. Couples must fight the beasts of routine and stress. So go a little crazy. Rent a limousine to go to McDonald's. Jump in a lake at three in the morning on a moonlit night. Reserve a honeymoon suite, the one with fancy mirrors and a Jacuzzi, for a weekend. Take up racquetball together. Send a love letter to your spouse through the mail. The sharing of fun experiences can be a bridge to rekindling a marriage.

SERVE ONE ANOTHER

Serving one another is a guaranteed way of reducing the tension and building the passion in a marriage. Look for ways to be a servant. Cook your spouse's favorite meal. Wash your spouse's car. Sweep the carpet.

FALL MORE IN LOVE WITH JESUS CHRIST

The most important factor in rekindling a marriage is for the husband and wife to fall more in love with Jesus Christ. It is the only way the heart can be transformed from self-seeking to self-giving. Without a vital and connected relationship to God, there is no power. It is like trying to see with a flashlight that has no batteries.

I don't want to mislead you. No matter how hard spouses try to reconnect with one another, there will be times when the distance will still be great. We live as sinful people in a fallen world. Selfishness is deeply ingrained in us; even the apostle Paul cried out in desperation, "When I want to do good, evil is right there with me!" We must be patient with ourselves. God is mostly concerned about the attitudes of our hearts, the direction of movement in our lives.

Lynne and I have recognized that we will have inevitable periods of disconnection in our lives. We have determined not to panic during such times, as we did earlier in our marriage. We call these times "commitment" phases. Although we know things aren't as good as they could be, we also understand that we are committed to one another for the long haul and we will do whatever is necessary to become connected again. This has greatly reduced the degree of whiplash between periods of connection and disconnection with each other.

If cold, disconnected hearts come to bed, there will be little heat. The mood for sex must be set in an attitude of treasuring and serving one another. As Rebecca says, "Good sex is all about two hearts that are in love with Jesus Christ. When a heart is filled with love for Jesus Christ, it looks for ways to serve others and express love." Washing the dishes for your wife or complimenting your husband on his parenting are just as much foreplay for intimacy as anything that happens in the bedroom.

As each partner begins to learn what it means to treasure the other and to give of himself or herself, the bedroom will begin to sizzle. An environment of love frees sex to be what it was created to be: the ultimate expression of oneness, a dance of intimacy, a celebration of *us*.

PART THREE

THE ROLE
OF THE CHURCH

CHAPTER 7

THE CHURCH
AND HEALING

A t the age of sixteen, one more girl has sex with her boy-friend. She is in love, after all, and he uses such gentle words of persuasion. She gets pregnant. Her parents, who are Christians, declare her a rebel, an infidel, and send her off to a boarding home for unwed mothers. Each night, she marks off the days until her due date, eagerly await-ing the arrival of her child—someone, she believes, who will finally love her.

At the age of forty-eight, one more husband decides to have an affair. His life, he says, lacks passion, energy, and direction. It isn't that his wife is so bad; she is a genuinely caring person, a wonderful mother, and a good friend. But he wants a break, a chance to revitalize himself, to reconnect with who he is. He buys into the self-actualization jargon, the hip Hollywood dia-logue. He will have his fling and then return to his wife. Three years later, eaten up with guilt, he tells his wife about his af-fair. She leaves him. Now, after his recent promotion to vice president of his company, he sits alone in a three-story colonial, next to the country club, crying when no one is looking.

Another couple, after thirteen years of marriage, decides they aren't right for each other. Over the years, they have drifted from one another, have developed separate interests, separate careers, even separate bank accounts. They hardly see each other anymore, let alone find time to talk. It isn't that they hate each other; it is more that they believe a new approach to life would give each of them room to grow and expand each of their horizons, to fill the void of separation. Mostly, they both feel they need some extra sexual voltage.

When they tell their two children of their plans to divorce, the children nod and cry. The couple knows there will be some pain for the children, but children are resilient, aren't they? Now, five years after their divorce, their twelve-year-old daughter still prays to God each night in secret, asking Him to forgive her for causing Daddy to leave.

HAZARDOUS WASTE

The examples could go on. Sexual sin has broken the hearts of those responsible; has disrupted churches, businesses, friendships, and families; and has destroyed the lives of our children in more ways than we can imagine. It is responsible, in varying degrees, for many of the serious problems we face as a nation: abortion, teenage pregnancy, broken and dysfunctional homes, child abuse, and rape.

One would think that in a society that claims to value reason the message would be clear: free love has brought us bondage; casual sex has had serious consequences; and the pursuit of pleasure has become a tour of hell. But sin never operates in a logical, unilateral, one-cause for one-effect fashion. You can't chart the destruction of sin. It is much like hazardous waste. Even if the box has a "DANGER: RADIOACTIVE" warning sign on it, and we try to avoid it, the contaminants might still work their way through the ground and poison the water supply. Then, anyone could be at risk.

Fueled by naturalistic tenets and the relativism of philosophy, our society has sacrificed personal responsibility for personal rights, loving relationships for self-fulfillment, and intimacy for orgasms. Increasingly, people are unable to rise above self-ish desires to opt for the greater good, something beyond the individual. The result is alienation everywhere: in families, among races, in hearts, in cities, in sexual activity.

SOME GOOD NEWS . . .

There is some cause for hope. Though sin often fails to bring people to reason, it frequently brings them to exhaustion. On numerous occasions, friends outside the family of God have confided in me that they're tired of living purposeless lives. They're tired of the treadmill. They're tired of buying stuff that doesn't satisfy. They're tired of achieving goals that in the end don't amount to a hill of beans. They're tired of sexual adventures that, after the initial thrill, fail to satisfy. If they weren't so tired, they would even risk dreaming a new dream, if a viable one were available.

More and more, people are looking beyond themselves and beyond the calculable, the provable, for answers. According to a recent Gallup poll, there is a substantial increase in spirituality in our society. More than 60 percent of those surveyed said that their spiritual interest has increased in the last five years. The number of college students who say that religion is important to them jumped from 39 percent to 50 percent. This openness to spiritual matters is good news.

. . . AND SOME BAD NEWS

But interest in the church—the body of Christ—has been steadily declining. Since the mid-sixties, the mainline denominations have lost more than 5 million members. I recently met in Dallas with two high-powered Christian leaders. One of them told me of his deep frustration with the church in this country. These aren't his exact words, but he said in essence: "I've given up on the North American church! I've just given up! It just doesn't work anymore. Not only are unchurched people staying away from church like it was the plague, but even believers don't believe anymore." This leader has decided

151

to put his time and effort into building churches overseas, mainly in what was the former Soviet Union.

THE "VISION THING"

Although he may be overstating the case a bit, few can argue with this leader's basic point: the church in this country is in trouble. And it is in trouble because it is not seen as vital or relevant to people's daily lives. This lack of relevancy and vitality has come about because of a more fundamental failure: the church seems to have lost the original vision of Jesus Christ—and where there is a lack of vision, the Bible tells us, the people will perish.

Napoleon Bonaparte once declared that imagination rules the world. Surely it is true that people are more captivated by powerful ideas than they are by charismatic personalities, legislation, or brute force. People will expend extraordinary effort, demonstrate legendary devotion, and sacrifice most of what they consider dear to themselves—sometimes even life itself—for a coherent, compelling vision. The men and women who have shaped history, for good or for bad, have had the ability to create and communicate a vision. They were able to capture the imagination and devotion of the people, inflaming their hearts and minds with passion and energy.

Martin Luther King, Jr., was one such visionary. In August 1963, on the top steps of the Lincoln Memorial, he described the dream that energized him: "I have a dream my four little children will one day live in a nation where they will not be judged by the color of their skin but by content of their character. I have a dream today!" "Let freedom ring . . . let freedom ring."[1]

Tens of thousands responded. They marched in Selma; protested in Birmingham; endured bombings, beatings, insults, and lynchings in many towns and cities—all to carry out the dream that King had so marvelously and powerfully described.

But Martin Luther King, Jr., wasn't the greatest visionary of all time. Nor was Winston Churchill nor even Abraham Lincoln. Those men weren't even close. The title, instead, belongs to a carpenter from Nazareth, Jesus Christ, the God-man who split history in two.

CHRIST'S VISION: TO BUILD THE CHURCH

Matthew 16:13–19 speaks powerfully of both the visionary and the vision, the man and His dream. During a private time of replenishment with His disciples, Jesus asked: "Who do people say that I am?" The answers came: John the Baptist, Elijah, Jeremiah, a great prophet. Then Jesus upped the ante: "Who do *you* say I am?" Peter did not hesitate. "You are the Christ, the Son of the living God." Peter correctly identified Jesus of Nazareth. He was the Christ, not some minor-league visionary.

Next came the vision itself. Immediately, Jesus Christ, the Son of the living God, described what He intended to do: "I will build my church, and the gates of Hades will not overcome it." His vision? To build the church. One redeemed, transformed heart at a time, He would establish a community of believers. His vision was like none that appeared before Him, and none after.

Although His vision was countercultural, Jesus did not intend that it be implemented by the typical means of revolutionary power: weapons, politics, or even religion. Instead, it would be realized through a community of people who would live on the earth under the direct rule of God.

In this community each individual would honor God with heart, soul, mind, and strength. Each person would know that he or she mattered to God and would be deeply touched by the love and grace of God. Each person would be drawn to the character of God, humbled by His holiness, melted by His tenderness, awed by His power, and comforted by His companionship. The community would willingly obey and worship Him.

The people of this community would be radically devoted to one another. The rich would make sure the poor were fed. The strong would bear up the weak. The mature would disciple the immature. The faithful would restore those who had fallen. Love, the giving of oneself for the benefit of another, would reign in each servant's heart.

Each person would use his special gifts and talents to serve the others in the community and would feel valued and useful. Each person would have a unique, but critical, role to play in the life of the community and would respect the others in that community. Creative interdependence combined with oneness among well-developed individuals would be the rule, as the people experienced the thrill of making a difference in the world outside the church.

The love and respect and intimacy and serving and sharing among the persons in this community would be so attractive, people on the outside would press up and say, "I'd give anything to be part of a community like that. That's what I'm looking for: a community where people embrace one another with sincere hearts." And the people inside that community would do everything in their power to draw in those outside.

That is what happened in the first community of Christians. For three years, Jesus went from city to city, describing His vision. And the vision caught on. Sometimes the authority with which He spoke moved people to silence. Sometimes the power and vast scope of His vision was difficult to grasp; it overloaded people's imaginations and overwhelmed their hearts. Sometimes the vision prompted those with power, the religious leaders who didn't want to share the pie, to hate Him and plot to kill Him.

For the church to become effective again at redeeming the culture, it must establish afresh the vision of renewed communities of God.

But as the vision unfolded it caused the hearts of the people to soar and their thinking to expand. They were no longer to be spectators in the drama of life; they were called to be players— and they wanted to be. They came to understand that following Jesus' vision was the highest calling anyone could pursue. It was the most truth-filled, compelling, God-glorifying, people-helping vision that could be imagined. It was (and is) fresh and creative and even a bit dangerous. Its implications extended beyond earth into eternity.

The church, brought into being by the power of the Holy Spirit at Pentecost, became a genuine community of God. The members of the church truly loved God with heart, mind, soul, and strength. Within the community, they loved, served, and gave of themselves one to another for the building up of the body. Outside the community, they offered an attractive alternative to life in a decadent Roman culture marked by rampant sexual sin.

"CHURCH LIFE": TOO OFTEN THE ULTIMATE OXYMORON

Some two thousand years after the birth of that dynamic community of God, a small group of believers was getting ready to start a church in the northwest suburbs of Chicago. They decided to go door-to-door throughout the community with a survey. Their first question was, "Do you actively attend a local church?" If the answer was "Yes," they thanked the respondent for his or her help and went to the next house. If the person said, "No, we don't go to church," they asked him why. The results were astonishing. Some of the most frequent responses:

- Church is irrelevant to my daily life
- Church is lifeless, boring, and predictable
- The pastor preaches *down at* me, instead of *to* me
- There's too much talk about money

I was a part of that group of believers, and I was heartbroken by the responses given to that survey. I vowed, before God, never to allow our church to be boring or irrelevant. If the vision of Jesus Christ is true (and it is), then church should be the most dynamic, compassionate, challenging, and relevant place on planet Earth.

What the people we surveyed were saying was that the church has lost its ability to challenge the culture, to be an alternative community in a world rocked by sin. Instead, the church has been willing to settle for merely getting along. In ancient Israel, people fashioned idols with their own hands and worshiped them instead of the almighty, awesome, holy God. Today, the church pursues the idols of dollars, comfort, and titles. It measures itself by these puny standards, rather than allowing itself

155

to be captivated by God's love, grace, and power. It has traded a grand vision for small dreams. Rather than sending shock waves through eternity, it has settled for being a ripple in a mud puddle reflection of self-absorption.

When we, the members of the body of Christ, lose the majestic vision of Jesus Christ for His bride, the tendency is for the corporate church to shrink into irrelevancy and jargon. The violent, transforming power of love is reduced to a tame scream calling for judgment. The comforting yet overpowering force of the Holy Spirit begins to feel like a cool breeze at the country club. The church retreats into holy huddles where safety is valued, seeking to protect itself from the culture it is supposed to be redeeming. It disconnects from real life and scorns truth as irrelevant. When that happens, the church loses its voice in the culture it is called to heal.

RECAPTURING THE VISION OF THE CHURCH

For the church to become effective again at redeeming the culture, it must establish afresh the vision of renewed communities of God. When Christians catch hold of the magnitude of this vision, they will be less tempted to compromise and more inclined toward involvement. Every other vision will pale in comparison. The money-making vision, the toy-collecting vision, the pleasure-seeking vision, the ladder-climbing vision— none of these will seem noble enough, important enough, or eternal enough to capture the imagination and warrant the investment of life.

When the vision of the church is recaptured, it will set in motion trends that will reject a retreat into isolationism, compromise, and irrelevancy. It will unleash a penetrating, transforming movement of the Holy Spirit that will inspire Christians to deal effectively with crucial issues facing our culture, among them the crisis of sexual sin. Christians will learn to value their sexuality as one of the most extraordinary, powerful, and unique gifts of God and will reach out to those outside the church who need this message. But how can this happen?

TEACHING THE DOCTRINE OF MARRIAGE

First, pastors and teachers must provide clear biblical instruction. As people receive teaching from the Word of God, they will begin to see the enormous potential of and responsibility associated with their sexuality. They will learn that the sexual imagery used in the Bible to speak of the relationship of Jesus and the church, His bride, is the same imagery used of husband and wife. They will learn that the goal of the church and of marriage is the same: oneness, complete unity and intimacy. What happens in our sexuality, in some deep and mysterious way, reflects the relationship of Christ and His church. Sex is thus not a casual matter but is of central importance.

Clear teaching on the parallel between the sexual relationship in marriage and the bond between Christ and the church will so elevate the marriage relationship that sex, the ultimate expression of oneness in marriage, will be seen for what it really is: the fulfillment of some of the deepest human longings. Once believers grasp the importance of the biblical doctrine of marriage, they will not be nonchalant or halfhearted about sexuality. They will earnestly seek to communicate the grand vision of sexuality as it is given in God's Word.

TEACHING OUR CHILDREN ABOUT SEXUALITY

Sex education, in its most healthy sense, will become a priority within the church. Teachers will shift the focus of their teaching from just the consequences of sexual sin to the potential benefits of sexuality, thus equipping parents to pass on this perspective to their children. Teaching the next generation to avoid sexual sin will be given an important place but will be secondary to preparing them for sexuality within marriage. Teaching God's design for sexuality will build in them the strength to resist being "blown here and there" by street teaching and give them the strength to resist sexual sin.

GIVING IMPORTANCE TO SEXUALITY ISSUES
IN PRE-MARRIAGE COUNSELING AND TEACHING

Sex education in the church will not be limited to instruction of our children. When Christians begin to understand the power of God's vision for sexuality, they will make teaching on this subject available to persons at all age levels. Marriage preparation in the church, for example, will be rigorous, challenging, and, at the same time, unmerciful. One of the signs of a healthy church will be the rejection of premature or ill-advised requests for marriage.

The questions asked of those considering marriage will be insistent: Are you presently involved in sexual sin? Are you both Christians? What are the odds that your marriage will last? Are you carrying emotional or spiritual baggage? What are your backgrounds and learned styles of relating? What do you expect out of marriage and sex?

The community of believers will recognize that if sexuality is truly designed to be a reflection of the deep kind of intimacy between Christ and the church, then the church must do everything in its power to make sure that those entering into the marriage relationship have the best possible chance of fulfilling that awesome responsibility.

Marriage enrichment classes, taught by gifted vision-casters, will devote substantial time to studying sexuality. Teaching will be tailored to each era of the sexual journey and will answer questions such as these: How do you handle sexual temptation during the sexually vulnerable years of middle age? Is it possible to place too much emphasis on sex during the early years of a marriage? Why, during the first year of marriage, do some husbands not feel sexually connected to their wives, even though they share a great deal of passion? There will be a recognition within the church that learning about sexuality is a lifelong process and critical to ongoing personal maturity.

TEACHING SEX EDUCATION IN THE CONTEXT
OF A CHRISTIAN PERSPECTIVE ON ALL OF LIFE

Sex education in the church will go beyond merely imparting knowledge. The title of a book on sexual wisdom in this context would not be "7 Steps to Better Intercourse." Rather, sexual instruction will be integrated into a Christian worldview that seeks to answer the the questions, Who is God? How does He want us to live? How do I fit into His plan? And where does the sexual design God ordained fit into the overall scheme of things?

By developing a Christian perspective on all of life, the community of believers will learn how to think—to integrate and analyze information—biblically. Through this process of thinking, knowledge will become wisdom and Christians will truly grow up into the Head, which is Christ. As that happens, God will abundantly bless their sexual lives.

DEVELOPING MATURITY OF RELATIONSHIP

But knowing and speaking the truth will not be enough. Preparing the people of God for service, maturity, and action involves more than their knowing sound doctrine. Church leaders must also focus on the process of relationships, those messy, inefficient encounters between fallen individuals who experience inward battles between self-sufficiency and self-giving.

That is where the rubber meets the road. Truth must be practiced in love. The Bible is emphatic about this. John, the disciple whom Jesus loved, states clearly: "The man who says, 'I know him [Christ],' but does not do what he commands is a liar, and the truth is not in him. But if anyone obeys his word, God's love is truly made complete in him" (1 John 2:4–5).

Truth must be made flesh through loving relationships. People today hunger for intimacy and a sense of being connected to other persons. Nor is it only unbelievers who face the loneliness. Christians are also deeply affected. Nuclear families have often exploded into pieces, neighbors come and go every few years, and friends who know one's entire personal history are rare, if not nonexistent.

Pastors committed to the vision of Jesus Christ must call the Christian community to a radical countercultural kind of love, especially when it comes to sexuality. They must remind believers of a concept expressed at many points in this book: that God designed sex to be the ultimate expression of love, the dance of intimacy.

If we want to learn the language of relationships, what better place to start than in our sexuality? The institution of marriage allows each person, in a safe environment of lifelong commitment, to learn how to love. It is often dirty work. It means daily dying to self. The part of us that seeks to live by selfish desires must be crucified many times.

The process of sexual maturity involves such death. As we learn to live in Christ, we free ourselves to give to others. As we come to understand through the relationship of marriage that sex is not just a physical coupling but a self-giving path of love, trust, commitment, and respect, then true intimacy has the opportunity to mark all of our relationships, not just the sexual aspect of marriage. This intimate, self-giving expression will carry over into our attitudes and actions toward friends, neighbors, and family members.

A GLORIOUS COMMUNITY

When truth is practiced in love, the result is unity. Listen to the language of Ephesians 4:16: "From him [Christ] the whole body, joined and held together by every supporting ligament, grows and builds itself up in love, as each part does its work." There is here a sense of virility, synchronism, precision, and power. The body not only works, but it is grace in action. It is beauty to behold.

As the vision of Jesus Christ for the church is recovered, the threads of responsiveness and trust will reweave the fabric of the church into a brilliant display of God's holiness, grace, and power. As the church anchors itself in truth and moves in love, it will become what it was meant to be: a countercultural, redemptive, transforming community that begs to be reckoned with.

POWERFULLY IMPACTING THE SOCIETY

Then, and only then, will the church powerfully impact the society. When the vision of the church is cast and caught, it will offer a vital alternative to those living in a dying culture. When the church is thus renewed, it will automatically gain a sense of relevancy. When seekers are genuinely attracted to a community of believers, they can't help but be curious about the truth that motivates the community and the power that energizes it.

If the Christian community will continue to look for fresh ways to create a safe place for unbelievers to hear the dangerous and life-transforming message of the Word of God, it will become increasingly effective in outreach and evangelism. It will provide seekers the opportunity, in an environment of anonymity and freedom from possible embarrassment, to discover answers to spiritual questions: Who is Jesus Christ? What really is the Bible? What is the Christian life all about? What does it mean to be born again?

This Christian community will also demonstrate, in word and action, the wisdom of the Bible about how to handle anger, disappointment, money, power, and sex. It will show seekers that Jesus' promise of abundant life applies not to some ethereal otherworldly existence, but to the real world of broken bones, uncontrolled lust, and shattered dreams.

BECOMING CONNECTORS

Before the Christian sets one foot on the battlefield discussed in this book he must know what God says about sex. That sounds obvious, but many Christians are woefully ignorant of what the Bible actually teaches. We cannot just assume that we know our own language—the words of Holy Scripture—with any depth and precision.

Even when we apply our best efforts to effectively communicate what the Bible has to say about sex, we can only do so much. There is a point beyond which regeneration really is necessary to understanding.

A deeper knowledge of what the Bible says is absolutely critical. It must always be our starting and finishing point. If we

161

fail to understand God's design for sex, for example, how can we hope to experience the promised joy of sexual purity and intimacy? We cannot practice and "translate" sexual truth if we do not know what it is.

We must commit ourselves to an active and never-ending study of biblical knowledge; we must shape our worldview with diligence and a commitment to the Word of God as the inerrant truth. Then we must live out what we believe.

The Bible then becomes the reference point for all our thinking. Through it, we filter all other information, in order to discern truth clearly and see more accurately the world in which we live.

Without the reality of Jesus Christ transforming the hearts and minds of those to whom we speak, there is no hope of redeeming our culture from the devastating attitudes and consequences of sexual sin. It takes spiritual people to understand spiritual truths, especially when so many words have been consistently bled of any kind of Christian perspective.

Our society has degenerated to such a point, especially in sexual matters, that many people simply do not have the moral underpinnings to understand what Christians are saying about sex. For Christians, for example, the word "purity" registers immediately, even though it is not always the standard for living. But what about unbelievers? Utter the word *purity* and, translated through corrupt minds and broken hearts, it means either (1) nothing at all, or (2) something incredibly stupid and irrelevant. They simply have no basis for understanding. We might just as well be speaking Hebrew through megaphones on Jupiter.

That is why evangelism, the process of allowing God to change hearts one by one, is so crucial and should be at the forefront of our efforts. Even when we apply our best efforts to effectively communicate what the Bible has to say about sex, we can only accomplish so much. There is a point beyond which regeneration really is necessary to understanding.

We must also exercise love grounded in humility. How can we, believers and unbelievers, reason together? How can we learn to speak in the penetrating manner of Jesus? To find a way to open the door to people's hearts and minds, we must communicate in such a way that people can hear, really hear, the good news.

There are several methods we can use to come to such an understanding. The most important is for us to develop and nurture one-on-one relationships with those outside the family of God. The motivation must always be love grounded in humility. We can only know the hearts and minds of unbelievers by rubbing shoulders with them.

Part of what we are doing as we rub shoulders with our unbelieving friends is to become "translators" of the Word, people who can communicate the truths of the gospel and the Bible's teaching about sexuality in terms people today can understand. The need for this goes back to the differing worldviews discussed immediately above and in earlier sections of this book. At one time the pervasive worldview in our culture was a Christian one. Even persons who were not believers themselves operated within a value system sympathetic to Christianity. In presenting Christianity to these people believers didn't have to start at rock bottom. But today, Christians cannot make assumptions about the thinking of people they are evangelizing. The Judeo-Christian mind-set, upon which Western civilization was founded, is no longer the prevailing worldview of our culture. It has been largely replaced by the talk show mentality of Phil-Oprah-ism. The language of Christians, once a vocabulary everyone at least understood, has become a foreign tongue to nearly everyone outside the faith. So we need to be translators.

We need, for example, to discover creative ways of conveying the meaning of *repentance* to the person, who, after committing adultery, was counseled by a secular psychologist to dismiss the guilt as archaic and repressive. We need to find new ways of conveying the meaning of *salvation* to a third generation welfare recipient whose hopes rise no higher than the next day's soap opera. We need to find news ways of communicating the meaning of *holiness* to the man who, in order to survive in the corporate environment, has been forced to drop the weight of his remaining morals. We need to discover a strong way of conveying the meaning of *faithfulness* to a woman who has been ripped soulless by a devastating divorce, or the meaning of *God the Father* to the victim of incest or to the child whose father has abandoned his family.

We can become such translators when we follow the example of Jesus, who made the "Word become flesh." Think about what that means. In God's design, it wasn't enough that the Word be merely spoken. It had to become flesh, the inexplicable transformation of the divine into a human context. Jesus entered into our world. He became like us, so that He might save us. He became skin-and-bone relevant to the places where we live our lives. He knew firsthand our longings, our limitations, and our craving for intimacy. With His own senses, He could see our sin—the deceptive places where we put our hope, numb our pain, and seek some purpose. He understood us. He spoke our language in a way that penetrated souls.

We are called to do the same. We must allow Jesus Christ, the living Word, to work through us to "flesh out" the Word to an unbelieving world. We must give flesh to our beliefs through our actions. This means that in our sex lives, for example, we must act in a manner consistent with what God has said about sex—for our sake, for the sake of the world around us, and for God's sake. Our impact on culture will be zero—less than zero —if we do not live what we believe.

Similarly, we must seek continually to understand the thoughts, feelings, needs, and longings of unbelievers. We must make a ceaseless and painstaking effort to identify with those outside the faith, to put ourselves in the shoes of the lost, and to truly hear and respond sensitively to the seeker's point of view. We must never become so "spiritual" that we lose touch with the realities of the world around us.

We need to feel the pain in the heart of someone who, despite endless sexual affairs, has fallen deeper into a pit of despair and alienation. We need to empathize with the heartache of a recently divorced woman, with two small children, whose husband left her for a younger woman. We need to hear the echoes in the soul of a person living life without purpose. That is exactly what Jesus did through His incarnation.

We must also grasp the principles that dominate the culture and provide a framework for making decisions. What are the forces shaping our culture and influencing our thinking, behavior, self-perception, view of truth, and sexuality? What are the motivations, the presuppositions, the theories, the spoken and unspoken values? When we understand the forces that shape our culture and influence people's thinking, behavior, self-perception, view of truth, and approach to sexuality, we will be better able to point them to the peace and rest of Jesus Christ. But if we fail to understand the prevailing perspective and the context in which people make critical decisions, we will be ineffective communicators.

That does not mean that we should compromise truth in our efforts to communicate and empathize with unbelievers. We must present sin for what what it is—the acid of death. But we must also know the difference between clearly and yet empathetically presenting the reality of sin and preaching down to the unbeliever in heartless judgment.

Nor does it mean that Christians need to sin to understand sinners. We are already quite familiar with sin and its devastating consequences. It means simply that we must seek, in the deepest humility, to understand how those outside of faith experience their day-to-day lives.

All of this has to do with connecting. It has to do with going beyond arguing someone into a conversion or trying to logically protest an immoral law out of existence. Christians are historically poor at arm wrestling. But much can be gained by quietly showing that, given the two worldviews prevalent in our culture, the Bible makes good sense.

If we can plant just a seed of logic and relevancy, we will have taken a major step toward shattering our culture's hold on an individual and allowing the Holy Spirit to set up His presuppositional demolition crew. Once that process is set in motion, the walls will begin to fall, and gradually (or sometimes suddenly) the individual will become aware of the precariousness of the foundation upon which he has built his life.

For over a decade I have tried to point an area businessman to Christ. Over the years, whenever our conversation has veered into the spiritual realm, I could hear the hinges creaking as the door to his heart swung closed. The Bible? A harmless book of religious myths. Jesus Christ? A wonderful human being. The church? A benign group of well-intentioned weaklings who need a weekly shot of something that normal people do fine without.

Simply put, this man seemed untouchable and immovable—until the birth of his mentally retarded son. Over the years I learned that the only point of spiritual connection I could establish with this man was to talk heart-to-heart with him about his boy. Did God care about the boy's condition? Would God's tender love for his handicapped son make the boy's life any more bearable? What were the chances of a miracle? Would the child be whole in the afterlife? What caused his defect? Does evil really exist in our universe, and is there really a battle going on for the hearts and minds of men and women? How does Jesus Christ fit into this cosmic struggle, and is a "chance" view of the universe really more plausible than the biblical view?

Before I knew it, we were having full-blown spiritual discussions comparing the two distinct worldviews. I could feel the Holy Spirit doing His ministry of conviction. But humanly speaking there was only one point of connection to that man's mind and heart—and that was through the love and concern he had for his son.

All of us as believers need similarly to lovingly identify whatever lingering tether the person we are dealing with has to God and then to strengthen that tether with biblical revelation until God no longer seems absent, distant, or absurd. No matter how challenging that task is, it is worth the effort—it really is.

When we are able to "connect" with a seeker there will develop, in the corners of his or her heart, a certain edginess that later will be defined as personal responsibility, and finally, sin. Truth, once allowed to penetrate, will always lead to a recognition of right and wrong. Hebrews 4:12 states that the Word of God is "living and active. Sharper than any double-edged sword, it will penetrate even to dividing soul and spirit, joints and marrow; it judges the thoughts and attitudes of the heart."

In this form of evangelism the goal is not to "convert" a person (only God and His Word can do that), but, rather, to poke a hole (even a small one) into the person's belief system to allow the Holy Spirit, through His convicting work of truth, to show the person the real nature of his or her predicament. That is where the fear of the Lord begins; repentance, then, is close at hand.

ONE HEART AT A TIME

As the church seeks to recapture its vision, Christians will become increasingly aware of the value God places on each human life, the deadly power of sin, and the underlying forces of evil at work to shape a world in which it flourishes. Christians will be passionate about entering into the spiritual battle with everything they have, which is nothing less than the power of God. More and more, they will marvel at the miracle of a transformed heart.

For it is only at the speed of one transformed heart at a time that the church will begin to fulfill its call to make an impact on the world around it. That is certainly true with sexual behavior. The lure and power of sexual sin is simply too great to preach it away, to legislate it out of business, or to believe that it will somehow disappear when people finally "come to their senses." Sexual sin will disappear only when a person comes into a relationship with Jesus Christ and begins, through faith, to tap into God's power for change, self-giving, and holiness.

JUDY

Judy is an example of the power of God to change lives. She visited our church at the age of thirty-eight, after two children, two divorces, and a broken heart. She came because Laurie, a co-worker, intrigued her.

Her fascination revolved, in part, around the fact that Laurie was happily married and, despite many painful circumstances, seemed to have a resiliency, even a sense of inner joy. Judy was also impressed with Laurie's openness: Laurie even told Judy about how much she enjoyed her sex life with her husband. Judy could tell Laurie meant it by the way she and her husband touched.

Judy, despite deep sexual longings, had become mostly numb to her sexuality. But that didn't keep her from trying. She often found herself in her boyfriend's bed, for who knows what reason. To please him, maybe. To keep him around.

Judy's recent divorce came after her husband left her for a younger woman. She remembers how her twelve-year-old son, on a bright Sunday morning a year after his daddy left him, took a baseball bat to a dresser mirror in his room. He said he didn't like the way it looked. She wished her fourteen-year-old girl would show some anger; she just sat in her room a lot, reading pulpy teenage romance novels.

Judy never cared much for church—too many "thees" and "thous" and not enough substance. But Laurie, one of the few people she knew who genuinely cared for her, made her curious. So Judy went. When she looked in the bulletin, she saw that the message was on restraining sexual desires. *Great,* she thought. *Someone else to tell me I'm doing something sinful, as if I don't feel enough guilt. Another church message about as relevant as a trip to Mars.*

But she was wrong. The message was mainly on God's design for sex, the gift of total intimacy between two people in a context of commitment and love. It touched her somewhere important and stirred in her a longing she hadn't felt in years, decades.

Four months later, she was still coming to church, captivated by the truth and relevancy of the words, music, and drama. During lunch with Laurie one day, the conversation turned to spiritual matters. Judy learned that she could have a relationship with Jesus Christ, who loved her very much and wanted the best for her. Later that day, she prayed as best she could. "God, I've done lots of things wrong and hurt you and lots of other people. I don't know what to do. I believe Jesus is the Son of God and that He died to save me from the consequences of what I have done." There was no majestic feeling, just a kind of quiet confidence.

And then, over the months, alongside a curious joy, the struggles began. She refused to sleep with her boyfriend, and he left her. He wasn't much, she knew, but was at least something warm in the chill of a moonless night. With his absence, there arose in her an ache for intimacy, something she had not experienced when her two husbands left her. It was as if her faith was reawakening long-dormant desires, which often dropped her to her knees in longing. She attempted to remain pure sex-

168

ually, but on one occasion she did have sex—with a guy on the first date, no less. The guilt overwhelmed her.

She decided to seek Christian counseling. It was there that she got in touch with the feelings of abandonment she had as the child of parents who divorced when she was ten. Her sexuality was, at first, a desperate and partially successful attempt to fulfill her unmet childhood needs for intimacy. But just as she was using others to meet her needs, so too they were often using her. The intimacy she longed for was frustrated by selfishness. Disappointment and then numbness set in. She always had to settle for less.

And then along came God, the One who seeks passion, devotion, and wholeheartedness. As she grew in her faith, she found herself with renewed longings that, through the perspective of her sinful past, she often turned into lust. She realized if she didn't come to terms with the sexual sins in her past and the forces that drove her behavior, she would be headed for more sin. Slowly and painfully, she began to understand the damage of sexual sin.

Judy committed herself to the principle of Romans 12:2: "Do not conform any longer to the pattern of this world, but be transformed by the renewing of your mind." Through a teachable spirit and a deep dependency on God, Judy descended into her sexual past: her pain, motivations, and failures. She got involved in support groups in the church and learned about repressed anger in children, destructive patterns of behavior, addiction, and poor self-esteem.

In each case, the group leaders cast a vision of what her sexuality could be, given over to God's design. That helped her move through the difficult issues. She learned how to tell the difference between love and lust.

Today, more than four years after she first came to the church, she is married. Her husband is a recent convert, also from a broken marriage, also with a history of sexual sin. Judy and her husband view church not as an option, but as essential. They are determined to break the cycle of sexual sin in their lives. Unlike other couples, they take nothing for granted in their lives. Because they are aware of their vulnerability, they are deeply dependent upon God. They have both slowed down, hoping to become more active in the life of Judy's daughter, now seventeen and struggling with her sexuality.

Things are not perfect with Judy and her husband. They still sometimes feel alienated from one another and experience the pain of disconnection that is the result of past sexual sin. But, some nights, when her heart is just right, Judy is beginning to experience a dimension of her sexuality that touches the deep recesses of her soul.

Where there once was sexual chaos, there is an intimacy that could only come as a gift of God.

NOTE

1. Quoted in James M. Washington, ed., *A Testament of Hope* (San Francisco: Harper & Row, 1986), 219–20.

DISCUSSION GUIDE

There are, of course, problems inherent to a discussion guide about sex. First, and most apparent, is that it requires discussion. About sex. Obviously, this is not the stuff of casual conversation between acquaintances; we're not talking here about motor oil, baby cereal, or the Chicago Bears. Sex, by design, is private; at best, a whisper between lovers.

Second, and shaded by embarrassment, is this fact: we, as members of the one body of Jesus Christ, must be accountable to one another. Even in our sex lives. And accountability demands knowledge.

So, in a discussion guide about sexuality, we have tried to balance the need for privacy with the need for accountability. This guide is designed for study with a small group, a friend, or a spouse. We recommend that the friendships be relatively well established and anchored by trust, love, and respect.

Here are some tips on how to best use this discussion guide:

- *Prepare.* The questions flow directly from the content of the book. If you do not know the material, the discussion will likely be stilted and artificial.

- *Be honest.* Don't try to think of the "right thing" to say. Spiritual growth involves being truthful with ourselves and others. Try not to hide behind shame, embarrassment, or pride.

- *Allow the Holy Spirit to lead.* The questions are designed as a guide. Don't feel obligated to work mechanically through all the questions. Because of the different dynamics of groups and individuals, some questions will spark intense discussion; others, boredom. Pay attention to the level of interest, the amount of discussion, and the passion with which the topics are engaged.

- *Be critical.* Always attempt to understand. Don't just accept something because the book or someone in the group says it's true. If you have trouble formulating questions, begin with direct and simple questions, such as, "What do you mean by that?" "Can you give me an example?" "I'm troubled by that statement—could you please help me understand it?"

- *Choose a leader.* The leader, preferably a person with gifts of leadership and discernment, should take the responsibility for guiding discussions, determining relevance, and making sure that everyone participates. (He must not be responsible, however, for providing all the "right" answers.)

- *Develop accountability.* Spiritual growth demands being accountable to one another. The leader might want to consider assigning each member an "accountability partner." Establishing one-on-one relationships in which the partners are committed to follow through on progress reports is often the best way to close the gap between wanting to do something and actually doing it.

CHAPTER 1
Sex and God

1. The authors state that historically Christians have had a difficult time acknowledging the connection between God and sex. We "liberated," contemporary Christians tend to deride such prudishness, yet in our heart of hearts do we really believe that God approves of sex? Can we imagine God watching us make love to our spouses? How does a person's perspective of how God thinks about sex affect his or her sexuality?

2. Read Jeremiah 2:20–25, Ephesians 5:25–27, and 2 Corinthians 11:1–2. Why do you think sexual imagery is used in these verses? What does the sexual imagery suggest about the relationship between a husband and a wife?

3. Without naming names, do you know of any couples over sixty who have a mutually satisfying sex life? What makes their relationship different from the run-of-the-mill?

4. As a group watch a television sitcom. Count the number of references to sexuality. How many of those references are in the context of God's design? Are any pornographic images presented? Is there sexually explicit language? Watch for subtle references. When the show is over, discuss your feelings. Were you surprised by the amount of sexual material, either positively or negatively? What effect do you think such so-called harmless comedy can have on a person?

5. What do you believe is the prevailing attitude in society regarding adultery? How does this attitude tally with the reality in the lives of people you know who have experienced adultery?

6. What does the recent emphasis on the use of condoms to prevent AIDS say about the present-day attitudes about sex?

7. Do you know of someone who is involved in sex outside of God's design? What is happening (or has happened) to that person? Have there been negative consequences? If sex outside of marriage is so dangerous, why are so many people doing it?

8. The authors state: "Our society's sexual decay will not be reversed without radical change. And this will be difficult. It will be like trying to stop a bowling ball hurtling down an incline. Gravity already has the edge. Education won't stop the decline. Nor will protest marches slow the downward momentum. New laws won't protect or heal us." Do you agree? Should we, then, as Christians, give up involvement in abortion protests, political activity, and efforts at biblical education?

9. How well do you think the church is doing in promoting God's design for sexuality, both by word and action? Why do you think this is so? How could things be done differently? How could you make a greater difference? Be specific and creative.

ASSIGNMENT: Individually or as a couple obtain a copy of one of the following from the public library: a recent issue of *People* magazine or any video rated PG-13. Write down any impressions you have concerning the sexual content of this material.

CHAPTER 2
The Two Designs

FOLLOW-UP: Discuss conclusions from the previous week's assignment: the sexual content of the magazine or video. What kind of sexual attitudes were promoted in those media? Were you surprised? With such a deluge of negative sexual thoughts and images, what can we do to remain pure? Is isolating ourselves from all of this material wise?

1. List specific ways that your worldview has changed since becoming a Christian. More specifically, how has your perspective of sex changed?

2. Do you agree with the authors that the primary front of the spiritual war involves ideas? Why or why not?

3. Imagine, for a moment, that you are present at creation. God has asked you for advice regarding the best method of reproducing the human species. Devise some alternative means of sexual reproduction. (If you are part of a small group, break down into smaller groups of males and females, then come together to discuss the results.) What do the different methods proposed say about our thinking regarding sexuality?

4. The authors state that it is impossible to have "casual" sex. Do you think it is possible to have sex with someone and not be involved at the level of the soul?

5. Describe a time in your life when you were highly disciplined in an effort to meet a goal. What kind of sacrifices did you make? How much did it cost? What did you learn about yourself? Do you believe that you are making a disciplined effort to improve your sex life?

6. Take five minutes and write out a two-sentence definition of the biblical concept of "oneness." Have the leader collect the definitions and read them anonymously to the group. What do the definitions reveal?

7. How often do you notice people around you (or even yourself) referring to the "latest scientific study" to back up what they believe or motivate what they do. What does this say about the dissolution of absolute truth?

8. Have the leader read from the first paragraphs of the front page of a newspaper or from the contents page of a news-

magazine. How many of the stories, in one way or another, are connected with people demanding their "individual rights?"

9. As a group, think about the number of television commercials that use the words, "instant," "fast," "quick," "easy," "now," or other synonyms. Try to recall the specific jargon. What does this language say about our society? Does it display an attitude that demands that things be quick, free, and easy? How could such an attitude affect a society's approach toward sexuality? Do you think such an attitude has penetrated your own thinking? If so, do you feel it has affected your marriage and your sexual activity?

10. The authors state: "In a culture reduced to scientific reasoning, what is efficient replaces what is moral." Do you agree? Why or why not? Give specific examples and illustrations to support your belief.

11. Read the quote from Dean Ornish on page 49. Do you agree that people today, in general, lack a sense of intimacy and community? How have the cultural values of our society affected your own capacity for experiencing intimacy and connectedness with others? What about your relationship with your spouse?

12. Do you know anyone in a New Age cult? Why do you think he or she joined—and what were the the driving motivations? Is this person attracted to your spirituality and your community with others?

13. The authors state: "When intimacy and community disappear from a culture, sexuality is often pushed past its limits. It is like a starving man who, finding no real food, eats a handful of dirt because, if nothing else, it temporarily fills his stomach." Do you believe this is why many people engage in sex outside of marriage? If so, how do you believe this could affect the way you witness to those trapped in sexual sin?

14. Can you think of any time in the gospels, outside of His interactions with the Pharisees, when Jesus was harsh and judgmental in His dealings with sinners? What does this mean in terms of how we should witness to others?

ASSIGNMENT: Pay attention to conversations at home, at work, and at church. Make a mental note of the following words or phrases, which have close connection to the scientific worldview: "efficiency," "the bottom line," "according to the results of the latest study," "forces," "what works for me."

CHAPTER 3
Discovery

FOLLOW-UP: Did you notice a prevalence of words connected with the scientific worldview? Do you believe that naturalistic thinking affects the the way people behave in our culture and, more specifically, how you think and act?

1. What attempts have you made (or do you plan to make) to educate your children about sex? Have your attempts primarily been negative, i.e., mainly connected with rules? Do you think a better balance is necessary if you are also to prepare your children for the positive benefits of sex within marriage? What do you believe are the most important factors in having an impact on your children's sexuality? In each of your answers, be specific.

2. Describe how you first heard about sex. Who did you hear about it from? What was your reaction?

3. Describe the first time you felt a sexual awareness? What did it feel like? Were you frightened, curious, cautious? What emotions did this awareness trigger, and how did you handle those emotions? Did you share those feelings with anyone?

4. What was your parents' style of dealing with you regarding sex and how to you think that approach affected you sexually? How do you think your style of relating to your kids regarding sex is similar or different from that of your parents?

5. Do you remember the first time you viewed pornography? How well is that image etched into your mind? What consequences have you experienced from exposure to pornography?

6. Recall your early dating relationship. How much did the physical aspect of the relationship play a part? Since hormones run so strong during youth, how can we protect our children from being dominated by their sexuality?

7. What are some specific warning signs of sexual vulnerability in our children? Once detected, how can we help our children deal with sexual temptation?

8. Your seventeen-year-old daughter comes home and tearfully exclaims: "Mom, Dad, I'm pregnant." How do you think you would react? How do you think you *should* react?

ASSIGNMENT: If you have children over the age of ten, try to talk casually with them about the pressures they face concerning sex. Try to find the answer to the question, "How much do your friends and classmates talk about sex?" If you don't have children, see if you can talk with a teenager you know about the pressures teenagers face sexually in their day-to-day lives.

CHAPTER 4
Passion

FOLLOW-UP: What did you learn about the sexual culture of your children?

1. In the previous chapter, the authors state: "God specifically created humans as sexually distinct, male and female. Certain masculine aspects of His image He stamped onto the man; likewise, certain feminine aspects of His image He stamped onto the female. Through the act of sex, the image of God, in its masculine and feminine aspects, is completed." In the story of Rebecca and her husband, there seem to be different sexual needs based on gender. Do you think this is related to the masculine and feminine aspects of the image of God? List as many different sexual needs of males and females as you can think of. How should this affect sexual behavior on the part of men and women?

2. Without going into great detail, relate your honeymoon experience. How have your expectations of sex changed since that night? Is this change for the good or bad?

3. After a fight, does your attitude and action during sex change? If so, how and why? During such times are you tempted to see sex as a tool to either release tension or manipulate emotions? How can you become more aware of these patterns of behavior and change them?

4. What are some safeguards you can take during the early years of your marriage to avoid sexual temptation? Are there specific preventative actions you can take to "affair-proof" your marriage?

5. Reread the story of Rebecca and her husband. Rebecca states that during the initial stages of her marriage she "began to think she was using sex as a Band-aid to cover deeper hurts." Is it possible to use sex as a sort of anesthesia? Have you, or do you now, see sex as a way of escaping deeper realities in your life that cause pain?

6. More than 50 percent of marriages in this country end in divorce. Increasingly, the message is this: there is no guarantee that the relationship will last. Without the context of

a life commitment of safety and trust, is it possible to take the risks necessary to have a fulfilling sex life? How important is a sense of security to the process of sexual maturity?

7. Have you noticed a connection between the vitality of your walk with God and the sexual temperature in your bedroom? Explain.

8. The authors state: "If we run (from sexual temptation) we will fail to deal with the real problem: how to deal with sexual sin. Wherever we run, even if it is to a distant state, we will someday be faced with the same sexual dilemma." Do you agree? How does this square with Scripture that says to "flee from youthful lusts" (2 Tim. 2:22)?

9. How do we handle sexual temptation? How can we avoid the steps of nurturing sexual fantasy? How can we discipline ourselves to obtain the underlying values necessary for sexual purity?

10. What attitude most consistently marks your sexual activity: love, the giving of yourself for the benefit of your spouse; or lust, the use of your spouse for selfish pleasure?

ASSIGNMENT 1: Have a quiet time with God and ask Him to reveal areas in your life where you have unmet needs. Write out those unmet needs. Do you feel you try to find fulfillment of those needs through sexual activity or sexual fantasy? How can you begin to deal with those needs in a biblical fashion?

ASSIGNMENT 2: Set aside some time with your spouse for a "sexual talk." Share with your spouse your discoveries about any unmet needs. Also, share sexual joys and frustrations, as well as potential approaches to improve your sex life. Be specific with one another. Attempt to deal with underlying motivations and not just the externals of sexuality.

CHAPTER 5
Transition

FOLLOW-UP: If you feel led, share the results of your time with God and your spouse concerning unmet needs and strategies to improve your sexual life.

1. Relate a time when preschool children provided a form of coitus interruptus.

2. The authors state: "The years just before middle age are a period rife with serious life issues, deteriorating resources, and surfacing problems. The energy of youth and passion are no longer available to prop up denial, hope, and illusion. In no other period in our lives are we so left to ourselves." Does this describe your life? In what ways do you feel the loss of dreams and resources? How do these losses affect you sexually? List specific ways you can nurture intimacy in such an environment.

3. Separate into groups of men and women. Discuss the following question: What is the level of intimacy in your marriage? Would you describe it as deteriorating, increasing, desired, or in a coma-like state? Is this a temporary or long-standing condition? If you feel less intimate with your spouse than you used to, how are you handling the loss? Do you feel, in any way, sexually vulnerable? What steps can be taken to restore a sense of connection with your spouse? Discuss ways that you might be able to talk to your spouse about your feelings. When finished, re-gather into one group and discuss the next question.

4. In the case of Rebecca and her husband, they chose to be patient with each other sexually. The text reads, "Just as God was patient, forgiving, loving, and challenging in His dealings with them, so they attempted to be of each other." Is this true of your marriage? Is it true concerning your sexual life?

5. The authors list five potential problem areas that often keep a couple from realizing sexual fulfillment. They are: selfishness, familiarity, emotional and psychological baggage, unresolved conflicts and unmet needs, and escaping into fantasy. Which area do you struggle with most and why? How can you better deal with these problems?

6. The stories of Cathy and John's sexual addictions may seem, at times, far removed from your reality. But do you recognize any patterns of behavior in their lives that have found a foothold in your life? If so, how can you protect yourself from falling into sexual sin?

7. Read the account of Nathan's rebuke of King David in 2 Samuel 12:1–14. What does this story tell us about God's attitude toward sin? How does this apply in our lives, especially in the area of sexual sin?

ASSIGNMENT 1: Come up with three ways that you can better serve your spouse. Implement them for (at least) the next week.

ASSIGNMENT 2: Think of a "crazy" date you had before you were married. Sometime during the next month, try to recreate that date. As you do, try also to recapture the feelings you had for one another during your dating relationship.

CHAPTER 6
Maturity

FOLLOW-UP: If you had a chance to go out on a "crazy" date, report the results.

1. Reread the story of Brad in this chapter. Brad seems driven by the need for control. How prevalent is the need for control in your life? How does it affect the level of sexual intimacy?

2. The authors state: "Brad is attempting to channel his sexual energy into other areas of his life. Sex, after all, is not just an act you do when you are naked and in bed. The full meaning of sex has little to do with the physical act, but rather involves the building of love, trust, commitment, faithfulness, and caring." Do you agree that single people can be "sexual" while remaining abstinent?

3. The suggestions of the authors concerning sex and the single person seem spiritual and biblical. But, in reality, is abstinence possible or even healthy? Isn't God asking too much of single people to do without sex?

4. How do you believe you have been the victim of sexual sin? How have you reacted: in self-protection, anger, or apathy? How has your reaction affected the sexual climate of your marriage?

5. The authors list six steps for healing from sexual sin. Review these steps and attempt to determine where you are on the road to recovery. What steps have you accomplished? What steps do you find difficult?

6. The authors say concerning the sexual journey of Rebecca and her husband: "Psychology, Christian books, marriage enrichment classes: all of these were helpful. But they paled in importance to a growing and transforming relationship with Jesus Christ. 'It is only as we are cleansed individually of our selfishness and sin that we are able to better reflect love to one another,' says Rebecca's husband." Could the real barrier to sexual growth in your life be spiritual?

7. Take five minutes and write out a two-sentence definition of "intimacy." Have the men, then the women, read their definitions aloud. Is there a significant difference between the men's definitions and the women's? If so, what does this reveal about the different needs of men and women?

ASSIGNMENT: Each person should devote a quiet time with God to contemplate what it means to "treasure" your spouse. Start by meditating on 1 Corinthians 13. Ask God to reveal practical ways you can begin to express more clearly the value of your spouse. Begin to implement those steps into your day-to-day marriage.

CHAPTER 7
The Church and Healing

1. What has been (and is) your current relationship with your church concerning sexuality? What questions were asked of you and your spouse before you were married? What priority does your church give to matters of sexual doctrine? Do you have anyone in your church that you feel free to talk to about sexual matters?

2. The authors state that "our society has sacrificed . . . loving relationships for self-fulfillment, and intimacy for orgasms." Do you believe this is true? Why or why not? What has been the role of the church in preserving biblical sexual values?

3. Do agree with the authors that the church is, for the most part, on the decline? If so, what reasons would you give for the slide?

4. What person is most able to inspire you? To get you to dream? What characteristics does this person have that are able to move you? Do you have a person in your life who is able to inspire you to sexual maturity?

5. What would you define as today's current debates about sexuality between the world and the church? How much real communication is taking place between believers and unbelievers regarding the issues? How successful has either side been in changing the belief system of the other? What are the alternatives to the current methods of "debate?"

6. The authors insist that the Bible must be "translated" into language that seekers, operating out of a different worldview, can understand. Do you agree? Doesn't the Bible state that God's Word, once spoken, will not return null and void?

7. Was it necessary for God to become human in the form of the person of Jesus Christ? If if was, what does this "incarnation of the Word" mean in our own efforts to reach people with the good news?

8. Do you think that Christians often look at a lost person as a "potential convert" rather than a fellow human being? Are we so anxious to convince people of the truth of the Bible, that we fail to listen, to empathize, to care? When was the last time that you hurt for someone you were witnessing to?

9. The authors go to great lengths to describe the depth, height, and width of the vision of Jesus Christ for the church. Have you ever been part of a group of believers that gave you just a taste of the beauty of the body of Christ? What was it about this "church" that impacted you the most?

10. How do you feel the church could do a better job of helping believers reach sexual maturity? How could you become part of such an effort?

11. Share a "miracle" story of someone who was delivered from sexual bondage through the power of Jesus Christ.

ASSIGNMENT 1: Think of the last time you were in a lounge or at a high energy, non-Christian party of some sort. Try to recall the conversations, body movements, and attitudes of those who attended. Try to get a grip on the thoughts, feelings, and longings of those who are without Christ. Take twenty minutes to journal your feelings and insights.

185

ASSIGNMENT 2: For the next month, say a short prayer (either silently or with your spouse) each time before you make love. Ask God to show you how you can better reach His ideal of expressing Oneness with your spouse.